FINISH YOUR FIRST NOVEL

FINISH YOUR FIRST NOVEL

A NO-BULL GUIDE TO ACTUALLY COMPLETING YOUR FIRST DRAFT

CHAR ANNA
CREATOR OF THE PLOTTERY

First published in 2023 by
Page Street Publishing Co.
27 Congress Street, Suite 1511
Salem, MA 01970
www.pagestreetpublishing.com

Distributed by Macmillan, sales in Canada by The Canadian Manda Group.

27   26   25   24   23   1   2   3   4   5

ISBN-13: 978-1-64567-797-0
ISBN-10: 1-64567-797-4

Library of Congress Control Number: 2022947178

Cover and book design by Emma Hardy for Page Street Publishing Co.

Printed and bound in the United States

DEDICATION

To all the supporters of The Plottery and to Barry,
my right-hand woman.

TABLE OF CONTENTS

 INTRODUCTION

Hello, writer!

You're here because you want to write a novel—you've decided to take the plunge and finally put the ideas floating around in your mind without permission down on paper.

Now, you might be a new writer. Never picked up a pen to scribble a story down before. Never stared at a blank Word document for hours. Never planned a huge universe of characters only to write down the first chapter and leave the project in the dusty attic of your mind.

Or—some of these things may sound a touch too familiar.

Whether you are a beginner or not, this book will teach you the easiest method for planning and writing your novel. How do I know this? This book details my very own method that took me from having a messy, no-plan draft to a fully cohesive outline and a solid first draft in just a few months. But you don't have to take my word for it, either. I've tested this method with other writers, too. I've worked as a personal writing coach with more than thirty clients over the past year and taught hundreds of students through my online Novel Plotting Academy. Some of my students have actually finished their outlines in a single day, and their subsequent first drafts only months or weeks after finishing the course.

I say this not to brag about success, but to show you that it is more than possible for you to achieve this result, too. And this book will be sharing all of the exact steps I take with each and every one of my clients—no fluff, no bull, no hacks and no false promises. Just storytelling, boiled down to the basics.

The thing about most books on novel writing is that they'll all tell you what you need to do in order to write a successful story. They'll tell you that you need a strong protagonist, you need internal conflict, you need a pinch point, you need an inciting incident, you need a hook, you need a beat sheet . . .

They tell you *what*, but they don't tell you *how*.

That's where this book comes in.

Chances are, if you've picked up this book, you'll know at least a little bit about storytelling. So, we'll focus way less on theory and fancy author terms and analyses of successful stories—because, at the end of the day, you really don't need any of that to be a successful author!—and more on actually *building your own story*. From scratch.

There is a very easy science behind storytelling, and if you don't believe me, just look at the success of each and every Disney story. They wouldn't be this successful had they not cracked the ultimate story formula. And then reused it over, and over, and over and over again.

Despite the genre—be it romance, fantasy, sci-fi or survival thriller—this book will teach you what is at the heart of every single successful and engaging book—internal conflict.

We'll use up-to-date media, popular shows, films and books across all genres to illustrate each part of your creative journey to make sure you understand storytelling as clear as day. You will come away from this book with a palpable knowledge and actionable steps to take toward telling many stories in your life with more ease than you ever thought possible.

WHAT YOU NEED TO KNOW BEFORE STARTING A NOVEL

You've made the decision—you're going to write your first novel.

Here's a comprehensive list of things you should have handy while embarking on this adventure:

- this book
- a writing device (laptop, computer or tablet with any form of writing software—or if you're old-school, a thick notebook and pencil will do!)
- an idea

This book will include templates you can fill in yourself while planning out your novel and your characters. You're going to learn exactly how to utilize these templates to create a solid game plan for your novel.

There are a few things I want to stress before you begin, so make sure you read the next few pages carefully. They will establish the foundation for you to tackle your project with the correct mindset.

CHARACTER COMES FIRST

If there is one thing I want you to take away from this book, it's this:

You can have a story without a plot, but you cannot have a story without a character.

You're probably wondering, what the heck does that even mean? Well, if you have a well-thought-out character with a strong motivation, your story will start to tell itself.

There are many books out there that follow no specific plot and simply rely on the characterization of the protagonist, and many of these books come from some of the greatest writers of all time, including Jane Austen, Virginia Woolf, Charles Dickens and Ernest Hemingway. This is why it's so important to make your characters a priority before you start writing and before you come up with any intricate plot. You need to know whose story you're telling. Character-driven novels invoke more emotion and more purpose, and even if you have a great plot in mind, it can only be made more interesting with the presence of a strong character to carry it through.

One way or the other, your character should always come first.

Never try to fit your character into the plot. Build the plot around the character instead.

THE IMPORTANCE OF AN OUTLINE

So, what is an outline, and why is it important for writing your first novel?

An outline, in simple words, is a plan for a novel that follows a certain storytelling structure. The structure we're going to follow in this book is the three-act structure.

You might wonder why you can't just sit down and begin writing straightaway. Some authors do it, so why can't you? Typically, these are prolific writers who already have an instilled sense of story structure and know how to pace their story naturally. But if you've never written before, or you've tried but were unsuccessful, plotting out your story is a must.

Here's what can happen if you don't take the time to prepare your story properly:

YOUR PACING WILL BE IMPACTED

It's going to be extremely difficult to be aware of your pacing if you write without a plan. What does pacing mean in novels? It's the amount of time you spend describing certain things, and under-narrating or over-narrating different aspects of your story can impact the pacing.

YOU WILL CREATE PLOT HOLES

Plot holes are small bits of the story that don't make sense in the bigger picture, and believe me, readers will pick up on these. If you don't plan out the reasoning behind all the things that happen in your story, it will catch up to you. This can vary from small things, like adding an idea or a hobby for your protagonist that you just came up with on the spot, and then never mentioning the hobby again; to bigger things, like writing a full-blown flashback chapter in the moment, then realizing later you calculated your characters' ages wrong (or didn't calculate at all), and the entire scene never would have been possible. These details will break up your consistency and ruin the story's believability.

YOU WILL HAVE A LOT OF UNNECESSARY SCENES AND/OR CHAPTERS

Not planning your story leaves you without a clear picture of where to go next, which means you could end up writing story lines, scenes or even chapters that won't end up being necessary (or useful!).

YOU WILL BE LEFT WITH A HOT MESS TO EDIT

I've seen this with my clients who approached me with bulky drafts they needed to make sense of. And you know what happened in 100 percent of these cases? We reverted back to making an outline, and they restarted the entire project with a fresh perspective. So, save yourself some precious time and choose to do an outline first.

YOU WILL BE MORE SUSCEPTIBLE TO WRITER'S BLOCK

Now, writer's block is a phenomenon that I don't personally believe in (more on this later). But if you start your novel with an idea and no plan, you will inevitably find yourself running into walls, getting stuck and proclaiming yourself a victim of the notorious writer's block. Don't worry—we've all been there once or twice . . . or a dozen times.

I know an outline of your entire story can seem like an overwhelming task, but that's why this book takes you through planning your novel step-by-step, and once we get to the plotting part, you're going to realize it's a lot simpler than you might have been led to believe.

You can certainly try to sit down and type out your story as it comes to you (even after reading all of my warnings), but you will likely get stuck much sooner than you think.

THE RIGHT MINDSET

OK, this one is a no-brainer.

You probably already know, on some level, that you need to be in the right mindset, not just as an author, but also as your own person, to be able to sit down and actually complete a novel. Ninety-nine percent of writers *never* actually finish their novel. And sure, I can argue that a big percentage of that is due to having an inadequate plan, or a lack of foundation or preparation—but do you want to know the truth? It's so easy to give up on a goal. And writing a book is an overwhelming and difficult task, with no instant gratification, which is why most writers give up. The main reason such a massive percentage never finish writing a book is that they're simply not persistent enough. If they were, they could have eventually come to the conclusion that they perhaps needed a plan, or that they might have needed to learn the basics of a story structure, or even invest in a class, a degree or a writing coach. All of these things then become obstacles that require effort to overcome, and most people do not want to put in the effort, and they certainly don't want to invest in a course or a person to give them these skills.

I know . . . it's all backwards. We're so hesitant to invest in ourselves, to believe in our abilities and persist in them, even if it's proving to be a little more difficult than we expected.

But hey, you want to know a good thing?

You just did it.

You invested in yourself by purchasing this book and by reading it. So, don't fail yourself, keep going! It will get tough at times, and you might feel that it's easier to just give up on this whole thing and go do something that requires less effort. That's when you have to persist and make that decision to keep going—for yourself.

There are ways to make this easier!

First and foremost: Make sure that you take the time to celebrate all the small victories. This could be creating your hero, thinking of the perfect name for them, nailing your story theme, coming up with your book title, working out that small plot kink that you just couldn't place, writing your very first page, finishing a chapter, etc. These are all things that you should be proud of. Keep reminding yourself of the progress you're making, and how much you're improving throughout this journey, and giving up will start to seem impossible.

Second, make sure you include self-care in your daily routine. And I want to stress the word *daily* because you should be doing something for yourself each and every day—anything that helps put your mind at ease and improves your health and well-being. Whether that's exercise, yoga, meditation, reading, going for a walk, soaking up some sun, having a peaceful hour with some coffee or taking a bath, find something that puts you in a good mood and helps you maintain a positive mindset.

And third, keep both your mental and physical space tidy. It's going to be so much easier to focus on your creative flow if you keep your distractions minimal—both in the physical space around you and in the clutter of your mind.

Before we get started, I want you to keep in mind that your first draft (the very first story you type out) is only a first draft, and its only purpose is to exist. It lays out the foundation of your story and helps you decipher which things are imperative and which aren't. Don't get discouraged if your first chapter is not exactly as you envisioned it. Make a note of whatever you feel needs to change as you write your first draft, but keep yourself going until you can confidently say you've laid the groundwork and you know what your next steps are.

Now . . . I think you're ready to get started. Let's dive straight into who your story will be about.

WHERE
TO
START

You might already know a little bit about the story you want to write. You might have the seed of an idea in your head, or you might have already typed out your first few chapters. If that's the case—awesome! You're already ahead of the game, and you've got something concrete to work with.

If you have no idea what you want to write about just yet, don't worry! I've got a quick set of questions and an exercise for you to try that could help you come up with an idea.

Let's answer the following:

- What sort of stories do you like to read?
- What sort of films do you like to watch?
- Is there any genre that stands out to you? Genre can be a great starting point.
- Now that you have an idea of the genre, think of the usual types of stories you see within the genre. These are often called "genre tropes." Write down any tropes you'd expect to see as a reader. You don't necessarily have to use these in your own story, but it's good to have an overview of potential story lines you can subvert and challenge.
- Is there any big moral or life question you'd like to explore?
- Can you think of a "What if?" question that might develop into a story? What if a mermaid grew legs? What if a boy bitten by a radioactive spider started to develop superpowers? What if the world ended and all that's left was your protagonist versus a bunch of zombies?
- Have you got an idea for a setting or a lead character?

Any of these things can be helpful in developing your idea, so before you head into this journey, I invite you to grab a blank piece of paper and write down absolutely anything about your story idea—whether you already have one or you've only started developing yours. Think of this paper as your mind's vault of messy, creative ideas. Don't worry about how it looks or whether it makes any sense. As long as you can recognize your ideas and find your way through them, it's good.

Now that you've got this lovely mind map, we can get started.

FINDING YOUR HERO

OK, first things first: Whose story are you telling? Who's the hero? Who's the central character you would never be able to tell the story without?

We won't jump too deeply into your character while you're still figuring out your story idea, but for now, I want you to at least pinpoint your lead character and answer these questions:

- Why them? Why are they so special?
- Are you confident they're the right person to be at the center of the story?
- What sort of journey will you take them on?

The correct choice for the protagonist of your story may not be obvious. This is something I want to stress, as I've had more than a few of my clients come to me with an idea and a protagonist, but working with them and talking about their story, we ended up choosing an entirely different lead. Why? Because it made the story stronger, it made it more interesting, and it gave them a chance to use a more challenging creative approach to the story, such as limiting their narrative viewpoint to a single character and thinking harder about how to include subplots through that character's eyes only.

So, don't think about the most obvious choice for your hero, don't think about how he or she fits into the genre and what the usual heroes are like in this genre. Instead, think about which of your characters has the most to explore, the most to overcome, the most interesting voice and the most relatable flaws and qualities to your reader.

When thinking about the journey of your protagonist, it's not a physical journey, and not a plot-driven journey. But a journey of emotional growth.

HAVE MORE THAN ONE PROTAGONIST?

You might go into your story with the idea of having several protagonists or even several POVs (points of view or narrative perspectives) in the story. This is something I see a lot of writers do without thinking through whether an additional POV will actually work for their story and enhance it. Do you actually need several POVs to tell the story you have in mind?

Several POVs can be great in these situations:

- When all of the narrative characters are equally important
- When these characters have a fully fleshed-out story that needs to be told from their respective perspectives, and they each have a fleshed-out character journey (see page 43)
- When the characters don't interact with each other and their story lines are kept separate but connected (for example, their stories set in different times at the same place, or different places at the same time)

In contrast, there are also many reasons that focusing on one protagonist can make your story stronger:

- You'll have one consistent narrative voice throughout the whole book
- You'll establish a sense of familiarity and connection to your readers
- You'll make it easier for your readers to relate to the voice that's telling the story
- It will give you more creative challenges to portray other characters

STORY PURPOSE, THEME AND GENRE

In this section, we're going to take a look at the three big elements of story foundations:

- Story purpose
- Story themes
- Genre

STORY PURPOSE

Having a clear purpose to your story is something you don't want to underestimate. I also like to call the purpose of your story the **story question**.

When you actually have a clear idea of what the *deeper* meaning of your story is, everything is going to be a whole lot easier to figure out. Here's something to understand: Stories are not here simply for our entertainment. Subconsciously, every reader is seeking to take away a moral message, to learn something or connect with the characters and author in one way or another.

The purpose of your story, or the story question, should be something you're purposeful with (see what I did there?). Why? Because your plot and your characters should all be feeding into your purpose, and so the clearer you are with the purpose, the clearer you will be with your plot.

Determining a story question can sometimes be a lengthy process, and there are writers who never really predetermine it but instead let it develop naturally. This is possible, of course, but I highly recommend you think about your story question consciously, because it will make the rest of your story stronger.

Ask yourself the following questions:

- Why am I telling this story?
- What am I trying to express?
- What do I want the reader to take away?
- What is the big question I'm asking with this story?
- Can I answer this question right now? (Sometimes, you'll need to actually write the book first to be able to answer the story question.)

STORY THEMES

Now, I used to talk about story question, purpose and theme all interchangeably. And that's totally fine—you don't always need to think further on your themes if you have your main story question. But here's where I'll make a distinction: You should really only have one main story question, but you can have a whole array of themes within one project.

What actually is a theme? A theme is an underlying topic of your project—it's a topic of interest you're trying to tackle through your characters and through your plot. You could say the culmination of your themes is what your story is actually about.

Here are some differences between plots and their themes:

FRANKENSTEIN
Plot: Victor Frankenstein assembles an artificial man and releases him into the world.
Story Question: How long can you be deemed a monster before you actually become one?
Themes: Nature versus nurture, abandonment issues, outward appearances

THE HANDMAID'S TALE
Plot: June must find her daughter and escape the Republic of Gilead.
Story Question: How much could the world change if we legally controlled reproductive rights?
Themes: Gender inequality, maternal bond, female strength

IF WE WERE VILLAINS
Plot: Oliver recalls a murder within his group of friends at the acting academy.
Story Question: Can we break out of the roles we're expected to play in our lives?
Themes: Betrayal, coming of age, self-discovery

Having a theme gives layers to your story, and it gives your readers a reason to care about what you're saying. Your themes will usually develop naturally without you having to think too much about them, but once they do, I would recommend stepping away from your project and thinking about how to best include them in your story with your conscious effort.

If you don't have a theme or a story question, or your themes are too vague, your story can easily fall flat.

GENRE

By now, you might have a clear idea of what type of genre you're going to be writing in. If so, that's awesome! If not, this section will go over main literary genres in a little more depth so you might find what suits your idea best. Each genre will also have a suggested typical word count.

Before we jump in, remember that your novel doesn't have to be one single genre. It can be a mix of two or more genres. It can be one main genre with elements pulled from other genres. Or it can be general, literary or contemporary fiction (page 28). Either way, you want to try to be as clear as you possibly can about which genre(s) your novel is. It can be difficult sometimes to actually decide which category your book should fit into, so let's review them now.

Fantasy (90,000–120,000 Words)

Fantasy is a genre in which you'll find books such as *The Lord of the Rings*, *Game of Thrones*, *Six of Crows* and *Book of Night*. The great thing about fantasy is you can get really creative, because there really are no limits beyond those you put on yourself. Of course, fantasy is a lot stronger with limits, so take care not to make everything possible in your world.

Speaking of worlds, most types of fantasy require intricate world-building. This means you'll have to spend some time in your planning process to think through all the rules of your world, its history and society.

This is a genre where you could see themes and tropes such as the chosen one, quests and journeys, powerful superheroes, supernatural characters, hidden worlds, dragons and other mythical creatures, fables, etc.

Subgenres:

- Urban/Contemporary Fantasy
- Magical Realism
- Dark Fantasy
- Young Adult Fantasy
- Fairy Tale
- Medieval
- Historical

Sci-Fi (90,000–120,000 Words)

Sci-fi is a genre in which you'll find books such as *I, Robot*, *Frankenstein* and *1984*. This genre allows your readers to look into the future and imagine what it might be like. Keep in mind, sci-fi is a genre that's extremely research-heavy, because your readers will expect story lines that are grounded in plausible science.

This is where you might see themes and tropes such as the end of the world, exploring space or different planets, advanced technology, world domination, dystopian societies, etc.

Subgenres:
- Alien
- Dystopian
- Technology/AI
- Space Opera

Mystery, Crime and Thriller (70,000—90,000 Words)
Crime is a genre in which you might find *The Thursday Murder Club*, *Death on the Nile*, *Five Survive* and *Gone Girl*. This is a genre in which you must pay special attention to reader engagement, and you should be actively anticipating in the thought process of your readers and introducing "red herrings" to keep them from guessing the mystery for as long as possible.

This is where you might find themes and tropes such as testing the line between right and wrong, questioning morality, the all-knowing but tortured detective character, strained family issues, closed-space/one-location investigations, the newbie detective sidekick, etc.

Subgenres:
- Cozy Mystery
- Spy Thriller
- Murder Mystery
- Noir
- Nordic Crime

Horror (70,000—90,000 Words)
This is where you might find books such as *The Haunting of Hill House*, *Mexican Gothic*, *Pet Sematary* and *Coraline*. Horror is a genre in which your reader will expect to be scared, spooked or disgusted. It's also a genre that can be adapted to a wide array of audiences; it all depends on just how scary and gory you decide to get with your details.

This is where you might find themes and tropes such as the afterlife, fear of death, phobias and the question of overcoming them, grief and loss, demons and ghosts, rituals, different dimensions, hauntings and exorcisms, etc.

Subgenres:
- Psychological Horror
- Slasher
- Supernatural/Paranormal
- Ghost Stories
- Young Adult Horror
- Haunted House Stories

Action and Adventure (60,000–90,000 Words)

This is where you might find books such as *Robinson Crusoe*, *The Alchemist*, *Life of Pi* and *Casino Royale*. Novels in this genre are usually plot-heavy stories with a simple but deep story message, typically driven by the concept of journeying.

This is where you might find themes and tropes such as underdog stories, journeys through the unknown, quest stories, found-family tropes, physical or natural antagonists, etc.

Subgenres:
- War Novel
- Spy Adventure
- Survival Adventure

Romance (60,000–100,000 Words)

Romance is a genre where you can find books sch as *Ugly Love*, *Pride and Prejudice*, *The Notebook* and *The Fault in Our Stars*. Novels in this genre typically explore a growth of love between two characters, and are generally more character-driven than plot-heavy. Writing a good romance book requires compelling characters with an interesting dynamic.

This is where you might find themes and tropes such as unrequited love, friends to lovers stories, grief and loss, coming-of-age, moving on and overcoming trauma and loss, loss of independence, toxic relationships, etc.

Subgenres:
- Romcom
- Contemporary
- Historical Romance

Historical Fiction (70,000—90,000 Words)

This is where you could find books such as *Lessons in Chemistry*, *The Book Thief*, *The Kite Runner* and *All the Light We Cannot See*. Historical fiction is any fiction project with a setting that's at least twenty to thirty years in the past from present day.

Historical fiction usually relies heavily on facts and staying authentic to the time period it lives in, and therefore it's important to note that writing historical fiction requires *a lot* of research.

This is where you might find themes and tropes of war, secret loves, inequality, class differences, poverty, global pandemics, thief and assassin stories, regal dramas, etc.

Subgenres:
- Period Dramas
- Royal Court
- War Stories
- Westerns
- Witcherature

Even after learning more about common genres in fiction, you still may not know if your story fits into any of them. That's absolutely OK. Beyond genre fiction, there is also literary fiction, contemporary realism and general fiction.

Literary Fiction (80,000–100,000 Words)

Literary is really an umbrella term for books that are driven by characters rather than plot. You can expect these stories to be set in the real world (though sometimes a metaphorical one), and they'll have a massive focus on themes and deeper meanings.

Novels in this genre typically deal with heavy topics such as politics, sexuality, family life, marital life, mental health, disabilities, addictions, death and so on. This is where you'll find books such as *A Little Life*, *To Kill a Mockingbird*, *Of Mice and Men* and *Where the Crawdads Sing*.

Contemporary Realism/General Fiction (80,000–100,000 Words)

Contemporary realism and general fiction are both different from literary fiction, and yet you could argue that they are the same thing. These two genres fit any book that is set in the contemporary or modern world and deals with everyday struggles and stories. Again, the themes and topics will be very similar to those I outlined for literary fiction, and these stories will be largely character-driven, too. This is where you'll find books such as *Before the Coffee Gets Cold*, *The Midnight Library*, *The Perks of Being a Wallflower* and *Normal People*.

In general, if your story doesn't fit into any genre outlined on pages 23 to 28, it's likely that its home is in general fiction.

Have you figured out where your idea fits yet?

Remember, your book doesn't have to fall completely within one genre: it could be historical with elements of horror, or a thriller with a hint of romance.

THE BLURB FORMULA

Every story usually has a premise. A blurb. An elevator pitch. What is that? It's a short, straightforward description of your project. Its job should be to set up your hero, the situation they find themselves in and the conflict of the story.

The blurb is the deciding factor between whether a potential reader will buy your book or not.

When someone asks you for a premise of your story, they might mean:

- a prompt
- a one-sentence statement that hooks the reader (like the short description of films or shows you'd see in the newspaper, the cinema or on streaming services)

It's great to have a very succinct one-line pitch of your story ready, but we're going to create your book blurb first.

It might feel a little strange to write up your book blurb before you've written the actual book, but I actually encourage you to do this early on for a very specific reason. The book blurb formula actually gives you a very quick overview of an entire story structure. So, what you're doing by writing this up before you start your story is making sure that your idea already fits into a general story structure.

A blurb is essentially a condensed version of your three-act story structure. If you come up with your blurb now, expanding your idea into a full outline will become a piece of cake.

Here's the formula I use:

WHO + WHAT IS THEIR CONSTRICTED SITUATION?

+

WHAT HAPPENS THAT PUSHES THEM OUT OF THEIR COMFORT ZONE? (INCITING INCIDENT)

+

WHAT IS THEIR EXTERNAL GOAL? (PROMPTED BY THE INCITING INCIDENT)

+

HOW DO THEY DECIDE TO ACHIEVE IT? (AND, OPTIONALLY, WHO DO THEY TEAM UP WITH?)

+

WHAT SORT OF CONFLICT OR CHAOTIC SITUATION DOES THIS PUSH THEM INTO?

+

END WITH A HOOK, A CLIFF-HANGER, A QUESTION, A WORDPLAY (YOU WANT TO MAKE THE READER EAGER TO FIND OUT WHAT HAPPENS)

Go over to your bookshelf and grab a couple of fiction novels, locate their blurb and try to examine how it fits or differs from the formula. Typically, you'll have one sentence that explains your protagonist's world and hints at their current flaw or struggle. Then you'll get a sentence that will almost always begin with "But when!" and this will introduce your inciting incident and send the protagonist scrambling for next steps. You might be told what they choose to do next and why that goal might become difficult. This is a nod to the conflict of their story. Some books will have a good hook at the end, perhaps a question that you can already assume the answer to, but it will make the story that much more irresistible.

When reading the blurbs, ask yourself:

- Does the author set up an interesting character whose journey you're interested in?
- Can you identify the inciting incident?
- Does the author tell you what sort of adventure they might take you on, what characters you might expect to meet or the world you might find yourself in?
- Do they hint at the biggest conflict their hero might stumble on?
- How do they hook you into the final decision to read the book?

THE SYNOPSIS AND EQUILIBRIUM THEORY

What is a synopsis?

We're going to treat your synopsis as a summary of your book. It's going to be:

- an extension of your blurb
- the jumping-off point for your plot grid

The synopsis is not something that needs to be perfect or polished, as it won't be a publishable piece of content and it isn't for your readers. Generally, a synopsis is something only necessary for an author and their agents and editors. You can think of it as a behind-the-scenes look into your story, where you can outline exactly what happens in your story and why, with a critical view of the creator.

I recommend a synopsis to be no more than two thousand words. That might seem like a lot now, but once you get to thinking about your book in a way of chapters, two thousand words could easily start to feel limiting!

You might feel more comfortable writing your synopsis once you've completely fleshed out your protagonist and the rest of your characters. That's totally OK. You can still write down the synopsis to whatever extent you're happy with now, and then come back to re-do it once you know more about your characters.

HOW DO YOU WRITE A SYNOPSIS?

Well, first of all, have your blurb handy.

Let's go over the general structure of a synopsis. What I use is the equilibrium theory by Todorov. It's a very basic beginning-middle-end structure for your story.

We'll separate your story into three parts:

- Equilibrium
- Disequilibrium
- New equilibrium

Equilibrium

The equilibrium is a proposed balance for your protagonist in which we first meet them. Don't be fooled by the idea of balance, though.

The whole point of their "equilibrium" state is that there is something troubling about it. They have an issue, a struggle, a flaw that's holding them back. The only reason they're comfortable with it is because it's their normal. But your reader should be able to tell that there's something wrong and assume this is something that may cause the protagonist trouble further into the story.

When figuring out your equilibrium, you want to answer the following:

- Whose story am I telling?
- What are they struggling with? What do they fear? What is their biggest flaw or insecurity?
- Where does that fear, flaw, insecurity or misbelief stem from?
- What is the incident that shakes up their whole world?
- What goal do they develop after this incident?
- How do they respond to it? Do they retreat into their unfulfilled life due to fear? Do they seek out advice? Do they completely ignore the goal or try to pass it off to someone else?
- Do they need another push in order to decide to chase this goal? What's the push they won't be able to say no to?

Disequilibrium

Disequilibrium is the point of your story where your protagonist's balance is broken. They're thrust into an uncomfortable and new situation that they keep having to figure out. They're completely thrown off from what they usually know.

Disequilibrium makes up the majority of your story, and it's all about novelty and difficulty. This is where you want to introduce all the obstacles your hero is going to have to face, all the secrets they'll discover, all their attempts and their failures.

This is the pressure your coal of a protagonist needs to go through in order to change into a diamond.

When figuring out your disequilibrium, you want to answer the following:

- What does their new situation look like?
- What is the new world they step into like?
- Who do they meet along the way?
- What is the first, the second and the third obstacle that they find along the way, and why is it an obstacle to them personally?
- What's their first failure, and what is the consequence of it?
- What secret might they discover in the middle of your story that completely changes their goal?
- How long will it take them to realize the flaw, struggle or misbelief that's holding them back from their full potential?
- Just how bad will they let things get due to this flaw they carry?

New Equilibrium

As the name suggests, the new equilibrium is a new established balance that your character reaches by the end of the book. The new equilibrium should always be different from the equilibrium, and typically this will be a positive change.

The new equilibrium is what your character achieves at the end of their journey, usually by completing their internal goal and overcoming something they've been struggling with since the beginning. This helps them establish a new normal for themselves, one in which they feel truly balanced and at peace—also commonly known as the happy ending.

WHAT ABOUT TRAGIC ENDINGS?

This is something we'll keep coming back to throughout this guide, but sometimes your story might not have a typical happy end. You'll still have a new equilibrium at the end of your story structure, but this might not look as fulfilling. Your hero might find themselves in a worse situation than the beginning, because they've dug themselves in even deeper, or they might simply be at the start of their journey, where they have to lose something at the end of your book—meaning there's likely a sequel to look forward to!

When figuring out your new equilibrium, you want to answer the following:

- How does your hero reach enlightenment?
- How do they become aware of the missing piece of the puzzle?
- How are they different after this realization than they were when we met them?
- How do they tackle their problems now that they have a different view of their issues?
- Does their goal still mean the same as it did at the beginning of the book, or does it become unimportant?
- What is the most important thing to them now?

Try your hand at writing out what your synopsis might look like for your book idea. Don't worry if there are blurry parts or some parts that are more detailed than others. Having any kind of synopsis is going to be very helpful when you move into your plot grid, and you're going to thank yourself for doing this step. It can also really help get your brainstorming going.

VISUALIZING YOUR STORY AND WORLD-BUILDING

Let's think about the visuals and the world of your story. What does your story look like? What is your book aesthetic? What type of world is your reader being thrust into?

Here are some elements that make up a book's setting and aesthetic:

- Location
- Time period
- Props and significant objects
- Dressing styles
- Colors
- Weather
- Technology
- Nature
- Music
- Society and politics
- Legends and world history
- Influential figures and leaders

Why should you think about this? If you have a clear image in your head of what your book should look like, it's going to be that much easier to describe it on the page.

Find some specific examples in your story for each of the items on the list, and stick to them in your writing. You're going to be creating a feeling for your readers—an atmosphere where the world feels that much more real.

Having a clear grasp on your visuals is what's going to make your writing **a lot more immersive, realistic and authentic**.

These are the steps you can take to create a mood board and a world:

- Do *lots* of research on the types of topics you wish to include in your story world. Contrary to popular belief, research can be really inspiring and fill you with new ideas you would never have otherwise had.

- Print out images that remind you of your book and pin them on a wall or a cork board so you have the visuals in front of you when you write.

- Find images online and assemble them together in a simple Word document or a Pinterest board that you can pull up easily for inspiration.

Here's a list of questions and things to consider when building your world, especially if you're creating one from scratch. This is super important for fantasy and sci-fi writers, and it can be a great research list for historical writers, too.

Geography and Nature
- What does the topography look like?
- What is the climate like?
- What types of flora and fauna would you find here?
- Are there any supernatural creatures?
- What's the most valuable resource?
- Are there any dangerous or unexplored areas?
- What would a map of this world look like?

Society
- What is the name of your world?
- What countries, territories or cities are there?
- Who runs the world?
- What is the political situation?
- What is the economical divide? Are there any classes?
- Are there any minorities? How are they treated?
- Are there any recent or ongoing wars, and what are they fought over?
- Are there any popular groups or people who act as idols?
- How is crime handled?

Religion and Culture

- Are there any religions? What does the religious system look like?
- Are there any legends about the world?
- Are there any historic events that impacted your world?
- Are there any world secrets?

Technology

- What does the technology advancement look like?
- How does technology affect daily life?
- What types of revolutions might this world have had?
- Is technology accessible to everyone?
- How reliant on technology are people in this world?
- Are there any magical systems at play here?
- What are the rules for this magic system?

Daily Life

- What does a typical day of a commoner look like?
- What do people do for entertainment? Where do people eat, and what type of food is considered a luxury?
- What does a typical family look like?
- How are children taken care of? Where do they study?
- Is there any unique mode of transport?
- Do people keep pets?
- What jobs and occupations are there?
- Are any occupations favored or frowned upon? Is there a lack of certain occupations?

STORY TITLES

At this point, you should have a general idea of what your story arc looks like, who the characters in it are, what your story world looks like, and what the main message of your project is. This might be a good time to think about your title (if you don't already have one, that is).

Even if you're not 100 percent sure what this might look like, I recommend at least coming up with a working title for your project. Having a concrete name to call your project other than "my project" could help make you feel more responsible for it.

There are many naming conventions you can consider as a starting point when brainstorming a working title.

SIMPLICITY
- *The Maid*
- *The Alchemist*
- *Twilight*

THE ___ OF ___
- *The Adventures of Huckleberry Finn*
- *The Seven Husbands of Evelyn Hugo*
- *The Picture of Dorian Gray*

NAME OF PROTAGONIST
- *Harry Potter and the . . .*
- *Anna Karenina*
- *Moby Dick*

ALLITERATION
- *The Great Gatsby*
- *Pride and Prejudice*
- *Black Beauty*

INTRIGUING HEARTFELT LINES
- *Where the Crawdads Sing*
- *If We Were Villains*
- *To Kill a Mockingbird*

The next time you're in a bookstore, try looking in the section of the same genre you've chosen for your project to see what types of titles there are. Which ones intrigue you the most, and what is it about them that stands out?

A powerful title will usually be born from the idea or the concept behind your book, and it might already tell your reader what they could expect from it. For example, you'd instantly know that *The Haunting of Hill House* was going to be a horror novel about a haunted house, wouldn't you? You'd know *The Adventures of Huckleberry Finn* would take you on a journey, *Murder on the Orient Express* would be a classic whodunit and *To Kill a Mockingbird* would be a drama with a significant story message.

A good title will tease your readers with the genre, concept or theme that it might be tackling. It might be bold and provocative such as *I Am Not Your Perfect Mexican Daughter* or *The Dead Fathers Club*; it could be emotional like *They Both Die at the End* or *Orphan Train*; or it might be thought-provoking like *I Know Why the Caged Bird Sings* or *The Lost Apothecary*.

No matter how you get there—whether you write out the whole book and stumble on the title in an especially important line of dialogue, or you use a premeditated formula and research the most intriguing titles in your genre—you'll know the right title when you feel it.

HOW TO
CRAFT YOUR
CHARACTERS

You might have noticed this is the longest chapter in this guide book, and it's for a very good reason.

We already discussed the importance of your characters at the beginning of this guide, and I truly believe that the basis of any good story is strong characters. Really, the characters are where your story comes together, not the plot. Ask anyone who's been writing or teaching writing for a long time, which do they value more—their characters or their plot? I can guarantee most will say their characters.

This is because any story worth telling comes from a character. You don't start with a plot and then plop in a random person to lead it. You want to know this is the *right* person to lead it, and one that's emotionally connected to and invested in this particular story. In other words, they are the story.

Think of Joe Goldberg from the TV show *You*, the timid bookkeeper who stalks pretty women. You're there not for the story structure, not for the cliff-hangers, but for Joe. Because you know that he is intriguing enough to tell you the sorts of troubles he might get himself into and what you can expect from his story. That means the story comes directly from who he is.

Of course, the plot of the story is important, but it's the way you get to the plot that will really make a difference in your writing. Do you develop it out from your layered characters, or do you think up a generic story line and fill the roles with fitting stereotypes?

You can see which story will hold stronger. Now let's jump into your characters.

TYPES OF CHARACTERS

THE PROTAGONIST

The protagonist is your leading character, the character you want your readers to root for. They're the person who's going to take up most of the time on your pages, and might sometimes even be the narrator of their own story, so you should be very familiar with them. A protagonist must have an internal conflict and a character journey.

Your protagonist is the key to writing a good story, and you should dedicate a good chunk of time to crafting them, as they will have to carry your story. These are things to consider:

- They should be interesting enough for your readers to want to know more about them
- They should be relatable in one way or another
- Your readers should root for your protagonist's cause
- Your readers should be able to clearly make out your character's growth (or lack of it)

Other ways to make your protagonist stronger:

- Make them active, not passive. This means your protagonist needs to be the one making their own choices and pushing the story forward, instead of only having things happen *to* them.
- Be mindful of their flaws *and* virtues. It might be tempting to make your character super flawed, because you heard somewhere that that's what makes for a good protagonist, but you need to give them some good qualities as well. Your readers need to be able to relate to this character and root for them, and they can't do that if they only see their flaws.
- Relatable motivation. Give them a goal and a reason they're trying to reach their goal. This reason should be something your reader can relate to and easily root for. If your heroine is a woman trapped in an abusive marriage, this is a motivation that's going to speak to a lot of your readers, and they're automatically going to be on her side.

- Give them something to lose. Give your hero something that furthers their motivation, a stake they're afraid of losing. Going back to the previous example of a woman in an abusive marriage—one way to strengthen her arc and give your reader more reason to root for her is to give her a child whose future she's fighting for.

THE ANTIHERO

What is an antihero? An antihero is a protagonist who lacks the conventional attributes of a regular hero. They might also have entirely opposing attributes to a regular hero. This can actually result in a much more interesting protagonist than a regular hero. The antihero tips the scales of the morally gray area toward a darker shade. Their intentions will rarely be pure. A few examples:

- Jay Gatsby (*The Great Gatsby* by F. Scott Fitzgerald)
- Raskolnikov (*Crime and Punishment* by Fyodor Dostoevsky)
- Harley Quinn (DC Comics)
- Heathcliff (*Wuthering Heights* by Emily Brontë)
- Dorian Gray (*The Picture of Dorian Gray* by Oscar Wilde)
- Sabrina Spellman (*Chilling Adventures of Sabrina* series by Sarah Rees Brennan)
- Patrick Bateman (*American Psycho* by Bret Easton Ellis)
- Villanelle (*Codename Villanelle* by Luke Jennings)

An antihero might have a **negative character arc**.

This is something I briefly touched on when we spoke about having tragic endings instead of happy ones. It's quite closely related to having negative arcs for your characters.

What is a negative arc? A negative arc is a character's downfall. Instead of growing throughout their character journey and progressing, they regress or "grow negatively."

There are many ways to show a negative arc: character corruption, disillusionment or simple tragedy. But the one key ingredient I've identified as necessary for you to be able to come up with a negative arc is this:

Your character fails to achieve or become aware of their internal goal.

It's as simple as that.

We're going to talk a lot more about this once you start crafting each of your characters' internal conflicts and journeys, and you'll be able to easily decide which of your characters may have a negative arc.

Most protagonists have the natural predisposition to live through a negative arc; it is only through their realization of their internal goal that they make the right decision in the end. If you want a negative arc, you simply won't allow them to ever reach that conclusion.

THE ANTAGONIST

The antagonist, or the villain, is typically the person or force that *directly opposes* your protagonist. They should be at odds with the protagonist one way or the other, whether this is having an opposing motivation, an opposing external goal or a different set of moral values and approaches to your protagonist. The antagonist must be the central point of conflict. They're the resistance band your hero is going to have to push against.

Make a strong antagonist by giving them:

- **A set of moral values**: Just because they're villains doesn't make them exempt from having their own morals. What does this mean? Concretely, if your villain doesn't abide by any moral rules, that makes them weaker, because they don't place their loyalties into anything and they're just bad for the sake of being bad. A villain who has a code and sticks to it is going to be stronger and more believable.

- **A connection to the protagonist**: A villain should always have some sort of connection to the protagonist. This connection can be something material—a family relationship, an heirloom or object that ties them together. Or it can be something intangible or abstract like similar or opposing goals.
- **A strong motivation**: A good villain is defined by their motivation, and if that motivation is not strong enough, neither is your villain. You have to ask yourself: Why does the villain want this? What will happen if they don't get it? What is at stake if they fail?
- **Logical decision-making**: They can justify their goals with logic up to the point that you as the reader might even start to empathize with their goals. The best villains are those who make you doubt your own moral values.
- **A unique personality**: Just because they're a villain doesn't mean they need to have one stereotypical brooding baddie personality. Make your villains unique by giving them a different set of traits. The more relatable and human these traits are, the more of a conflict you cause between the villain and the reader's goals. The more unrelatable these traits, the bigger the potential for fear and intrigue.

NONPHYSICAL ANTAGONISTS

Don't be alarmed if you don't have a physical antagonist, such as a person, a monster or an organization. There are different types of antagonists who don't have to manifest as a physical person. Your antagonist might be more abstract like the weather (*Outside* by Ragnar Jónasson), a natural disaster (*The Stand* by Stephen King), time (*The Curious Case of Benjamin Button* by F. Scott Fitzgerald), society (*The Handmaid's Tale* by Margaret Atwood) or social circumstance (*Lord of the Flies* by William Golding).

This is what we would call **antagonistic forces**.

Even if it isn't one concrete villain, your protagonist still needs to be pushing against some sort of resistance in the story, one that is directly in opposition to their goals.

In Margaret Atwood's *The Handmaid's Tale*, June Osborne faces many such resistances from the general makeup of the new society to smaller physical antagonists, such as the family she's forced into servitude for or the matriarchs she must answer to. However, none of these characters can be referred to as "the villain" of the story. They are pieces of the antagonistic forces which represent the true antagonist of the story—the Republic of Gilead.

Think of the romance novel *The Notebook* by Nicholas Sparks. There is no concrete villain in this story, either, but the antagonistic forces are all the socioeconomic circumstances—the characters' families and choices that present an obstacle to the couple we're following and rooting for.

This is an extremely common concept in most books, especially those set in the contemporary world.

The things I listed above are all external forces that may cause a story conflict to your protagonist when they are trying to achieve their goals (for June escaping the Republic, or for the couple to be together happily), but this main force of antagonism can also be internal, which means the antagonism is found inside your protagonist.

ANTAGONISTIC PROTAGONIST IN LITERARY NOVELS

You might think it's a contradictory idea to have a protagonist who also shares the role of the antagonist, but I promise you it's really simple.

An antagonistic protagonist is the type of protagonist who **self-sabotages** their external goal by ignoring or being oblivious to their internal goal. They don't have any opposing external forces such as villains, enemies or even an antagonistic force. In simple terms, they are their own worst enemy.

The first literary novel that comes to mind as an example is *Madame Bovary* by Gustave Flaubert. It follows a woman who is continuously dissatisfied with anything life gives her, chasing an external goal that never satisfies her. Because of this, she's the main reason anything bad ever happens to her.

This type of protagonist is typically only present in literary novels (character-driven novels).

If you've ever had a really good story idea but were worried about not having a concrete antagonist, ask yourself whether your hero can actually fill both of these roles.

If your antagonist is truly just an antagonistic force or the protagonist themselves, then it's quite common to have some **smaller objects or persons of antagonism.** These won't be "the big bad," but they might help push your hero into some uncomfortable situations. They might represent the system of social injustice (like guards enforcing rules of a government system) or be minor characters who come into conflict with your hero on their journey but aren't necessarily the villain.

MAJOR CHARACTER

A major character is one who might not be the lead, but is still crucial to the story. They're typically very close to the protagonist—they might be a best friend, a love interest, a mentor, a parent, etc.

In most cases, the major character should have their own internal conflict and their own character journey within your story. This means you would work them out in the same way you would with your protagonist. Don't skimp out and don't think of them as any less important than your hero.

MINOR CHARACTER

A minor character is the type of character who might not be directly related to your protagonist. They might be their love interest's best friend, their teacher's child or their best friend's parent. These types do not tend to have their own arcs, but rather will **serve a purpose within the story.**

This is the main difference between your major and minor characters:

The major characters will have an internal conflict that will lead to a **character journey.** This means they'll **change** throughout the story. Your minor characters will instead have a **purpose,** but internally they will **stay the same.**

Minor characters are generally used as "devices" within your story, which means they are there to influence your major characters or change the plot somehow, without changing themselves. You can look at them as "complete" characters. They might have nothing to learn at the moment, and they feel comfortable with themselves, or they simply never intend to change. Minor characters can become major characters throughout your story, especially if you're writing a series, and this is easily done by giving them something to overcome.

But minor characters should always be used **with a purpose**. We'll explore what this can be when we start crafting your characters (see page 52).

The "Introduce Them Twice" Trick
For minor characters who serve a purpose to your major ones, you might consider using the trick of introducing them twice.

How does this work? Introduce them once quickly in passing—your main character notices them, maybe speaks about them with their friend—then give them a proper introduction the next time your character sees them. This creates a more natural progression of events in your story and makes your minor characters seem like less of a "purpose character" and more like someone who's been there all along.

THE PASSERBY
The passerby is a character who you come across in your writing, and they might have been completely unplanned. They're just there for the scene—they help paint a picture of your world, or they serve as an opportunity for the readers to get to know your major characters a little bit better. These are characters whom we'll meet only once or twice in passing. We won't find out a whole lot about them, but they will still make an impact on the story.

How Can You Write a Good Passerby?
Passersby are the type of characters who can easily become forgettable. It's not to say that when writing a passerby type your goal is to make them memorable, but if you feel like bringing them back for another quick scene, you will want your readers to remember them from before.

Say one of your major characters works in a bar, and there is a local who comes in for a drink every now and then. You're using this local to paint the picture of the town setting, or even to lighten the mood. If you call him Jerry and tell your readers he sits at the bar quietly nursing a drink before saying goodbye and leaving, there's a high probability that if you mention Jerry after one hundred pages, they will have no clue who he is. However, if you nickname him Blinky, the chatty neighbor who never seems to blink, and tell your readers he comes in for five double vodkas every evening, which he downs in ten minutes, and keeps interrupting your major character's conversations to give unsolicited advice, it's much more likely that if you decide to bring Blinky back after one hundred pages, your readers might smile as they remember his earlier presence.

This is called caricaturing. It works really well on small characters who need to be memorable or serve a certain purpose. Simply think of a starting point from which to build them, and then push into it as far as you can. While these characters can be heavily unrealistic, make sure you're not slipping into any harmful stereotypes.

And remember, this technique should be reserved only for the characters with the smallest presence in your book who are there solely to fulfill a purpose—like Blinky interrupting your major characters simply to push their buttons. These characters are great for writing scenes where you use The Third Character Trick (see page 119). Your major characters should not rely on caricatures, unless you are writing absurdist fiction.

Passersby can be:

- Servers
- Locals
- Strangers
- Bus drivers
- Teachers
- Any other character who might typically only be present in a small scene, and doesn't change your story in any way

You do not need a character sheet for this type of character.

If you have a dinner scene between two of your important characters and you need to introduce a quick waitress character into the scene, **use it as an opportunity to build**. Don't include a boring, stereotypical waitress who simply does her job and gets on with it. Instead, think of how she might serve your bigger characters, or the situation they are currently in, as an added conflict.

Are they discussing something sad, something serious?

- Make the waitress super bubbly, and have her interrupt them frequently.
- Make her unable to read the room, as she presents the overly long menu and makes corny jokes.

Are they trying to have a romantic dinner?

- Make their waitress grumpy and rude.
- Make her flirt with one of them.

Are they trying to have a private conversation?

- Make her chip in with her own opinions.
- Make her overhear something and repeat it loudly with interest.

Similarly, instead of using passersby for further conflict, you can also use them to tell us something about your bigger characters. **Use them to build up the characteristics you want us to know about your major characters.**

For example, you could introduce an older person who's struggling with their grocery bags. If you want us to like your major character, they can go over and help them; if you want us to dislike them, they can keep walking.

Or, if you have a rude service person, your major character might retreat into themself and feel embarrassed at the interaction. This paints them as a nonconfrontational person. For a more confrontational approach, they might argue back.

CRAFTING YOUR CHARACTER
THE BASICS

Let's begin with the very basics of what makes up a character. Here are some of the things you should know about your character:

What is their gender and sexuality? How do they identify? How old are they? What is their nationality and their heritage? Which race or culture do they come from? These are very straightforward characteristics and the basic information you should start to think about.

How do you picture them? If you're a visual person, the easiest thing to do here is pick an actor, a model or even an artistic representation of your character.

What is their role in the story? Are they the hero? The villain? The sidekick?

What is their role in relation to the protagonist? Are they your main character's parents? Their best friend? Their teacher? Their enemy?

In addition to this basic information, you might also include any specifics related to your world (especially if you're writing fantasy, sci-fi or dystopian novels) such as a made-up race, the fantasy creature they might be or a social group they might belong to (like the Hogwarts houses or the Hunger Games factions).

NAMING YOUR CHARACTER

Naming your character doesn't have to be difficult. The genre and setting should have an influence on what you choose to name your characters. You can also consider strengthening the name with some creative symbolism.

GENRE

Your names are going to differ depending on whether you're writing in the fantasy genre or the historical genre. For fantasy, sci-fi or dystopian novels, you have much more freedom over the types of names you choose or make up. However, with novels set in the contemporary world, you should think about where and when your story is set, and whether it's at least vaguely believable that your character would be named a certain name. Of course, allow yourself some creative freedom by suspension of disbelief (meaning you don't always have to be spot on with the fact, just close enough).

SETTING

Make sure the names you choose are appropriate for whatever setting you're working with.

- **Location:** Think about where in the world your story is set and how this might influence your characters' names and surnames. Which country do they come from, where do they pull their ancestry from?
- **Time period:** Names change and evolve over time as does the general vocabulary of humans. We don't speak the same way we did a hundred years ago, and we don't name our children the same names, either. It's good to research generational names used in your chosen time period. You're likely not going to name a character from the 1600s Sasha or Jayden.

PERSONALITY AND SYMBOLISM

You can be quite transparent with your names, too, and base them largely on your character's personality, their motive or their role in the story.

Here are some examples across other literature:

- Alina Starkov from *Shadow and Bone* – *Alina* translates to "light," and *Starkov* contains the word *star*, which hints at the character's powers of light.
- Rodion Raskolnikov from *Crime and Punishment* – *Raskol* means "a split" in Russian, and *raskolnik* is someone who goes against the beliefs of a group, which is the thematic question that the entire book is based on.
- Sabrina Spellman from Archie Comics – A teenage witch whose last name literally spells out the fact that she is, in fact, a witch. *Ba-dum-tss.*
- Napoleon from *Animal Farm* – The ring leader of the communist pigs on Orwell's farm.
- Desdemona from *Othello* – Desdemona translates to "ill-fated."
- Hannibal Lecter from *Hannibal* – A cannibalistic serial killer.

A good method for coming up with symbolic names is to translate some keywords that can describe your character or their motive into different languages (Latin and French are good choices for this trick!).

ALLITERATION

Think about using alliteration to help with the rhythm and the memorability of your character's name. What is alliteration? Simply put, it's using the same letter at the start of your character's name and surname, such as Peter Parker, Benjamin Button, Lois Lane, Lex Luther, Severus Snape, Sabrina Spellman, Bilbo Baggins, Stefan Salvatore and Jughead Jones.

This is an extremely simple trick that helps the name be more memorable and melodic in your readers' minds. It is also a popular naming convention for comic book characters and superheros.

Bonus Tip
Consider adding a title, prefix or suffix to the name for flow and memorability such as Miss, Missus, Sir, Doctor, Professor, Coach, Reverend, Junior, Senior, the second or the third.

CHARACTER VOICES

What's a Character Voice and Why Is It Important?
A character's voice should be just as unique as their personality. Unfortunately, this is often the most overlooked part of crafting a good character, even in bestsellers, and is one that is very popular for comic book characters and superheroes.

Crafting good character voices sets the foundation for writing good dialogue without too much effort on your part. So let's get into it.

The Protagonist or Narrator
Start with dividing your protagonist's voice into narrative and speaking parts.

Narrative Voice. The narrative voice is the internal voice your character uses as they narrate the story. This voice is used in all close narrative perspectives, such as first or third close person. We'll discuss this in greater detail in the Narrative Perspectives section (page 106).

Speaking Voice. The speaking voice is the voice your character will use when communicating with other characters within the story.

Why Is It Important to Make a Distinction Between the Two?
The way a character speaks to the audience is inevitably going to be a truer portrayal of their personality than that which they use outwardly. By separating the voices, you can add nuance and layers to the character without even trying.

Here are a few examples.

Imagine a character who makes witty remarks in his head about things he sees. He shares his contempt and his dissatisfaction about things around him. But then when he speaks to other characters, he's overly polite and kind, without one bad word to say.

How does that make us feel about the character? We can tell he's likely two-faced, and might even have a tendency to lie, just by the difference between the two voices he uses.

Imagine a character who speaks to the readers very clearly, is well-read and has a wide range of vocabulary, but when he speaks to others he barely says more than a few words at a time.

This distinction between the narrative and speaking voices could be a hint at a social anxiety disorder.

Other Characters' Voices

Each character—not just your protagonist—should have their own voice.

So, how do you actually come up with a unique character voice? It's up to a few defining factors. These are the things you should ask yourself:

- Where do they come from? Where did they grow up?
- Who did they grow up with? What were their parents like, and how did they speak?
- Are there any influences in their life that might have altered the way they speak? (For example, if they had an uncle who cursed a lot, this could influence your character to use the same curses.)
- Did they pick up expressions or sayings from other people?
- What is their academic level? Why type of vocabulary would they have access to?
- Do they have a distinct accent?
- What is their speech pattern?
- Do they have a stutter? Do they mutter?
- Are they quiet? Loud?
- What is their personality like, and how does that affect their voice? Are they honest and straight to the point? Or do they talk around the point for as long as they can?

Expressions and Sayings

Another thing that could enhance your character's voice is coining unique phrases for them. This doesn't have to be anything unnecessarily complicated.

Let's look at some examples:

- "The game is afoot!" —*Sherlock Holmes*, Arthur Conan Doyle
- "Big Brother is watching you." —*1984*, George Orwell
- "So it goes." —*Slaughterhouse-Five*, Kurt Vonnegut
- "Little grey cells." —Hercule Poirot novels, Agatha Christie
- "Why so serious?" —Batman comics, Bob Kane

Now, your catchphrases don't necessarily need to be one specific thing. It could be in the way a character asks a question. For example, instead of saying "Did you know that?" they could phrase it as "You didn't know that, did you?"; instead of "Are you OK?" they could say "You're not OK, are you?" This simple rephrasing could also give you insight into the way that character thinks—maybe they're the type of person who has a sixth sense for things like that, so their questions aren't really questions but confirmations of things they already think they know.

They could also make excessive use of a specific word, but phrase it differently each time.

In Wes Anderson's film *The Darjeeling Limited*, we hear Owen Wilson's character continuously repeating his reaffirmation phrase "Can we agree to that?" almost every time he addresses his brothers. He sometimes also begins his lines with "Let's make another agreement."

This also helps us to realize that every time Owen's character is trying to "make an agreement," it's likely a soft form of manipulation.

Where to Stop

As with all things, balance is key. Don't stick to these formulas too tightly as you still want your characters to sound natural. Writing is a creative process, so come up with your own ways to add personality to character voice. There's really an infinite source of inspiration around you.

PERSONALITIES

A character's personality should consist of their **virtues, flaws, quirks and internal conflict**. All of these things build up who they are and how they act in certain situations.

Virtues and Flaws

To paint a good picture of a morally gray character, you need to make sure their virtues and flaws **balance each other out**.

The most common trap a lot of writers fall down is attempting to make their protagonist flawed—they tend to tip the scales too far and end up with an unlikeable character the readers can't root for. If you're going to give your character flaws, make sure they do actually have redeeming qualities as well. We don't want perfect characters, but we also want characters we can care about and root for.

Examples of virtues:

- Good listener
- Sensitive
- In control of their emotions
- Kindhearted
- Polite
- Well-humored
- Talented at a certain hobby
- Optimistic
- Easygoing
- Conversation starter

Examples of flaws:

- Naive
- Self-critical
- Closed off
- Manipulative
- Selfish
- Self-sacrificing
- Ruled by their anger
- Overprotective
- Controlling
- Eager to please
- Doesn't think before speaking
- Judgmental

Keep in mind: Not all of these are so easily distinguishable, and it will depend on your story.

While "sensitive" might be regarded as a flaw by some, it might actually be a virtue for your character within the context of your story.

The entire reason I urge you to separate your virtues and flaws is so you can clearly see the balance between the two. If, however, you're going for a **black-and-white moral representation** in your world, such as a fairy tale, then you might lean more heavily into virtues for your heroes and flaws for your villains.

Writing morally gray characters has been increasingly more popular in modern fiction, so if this is your goal for the story, make sure your flaws don't outweigh the virtues, or your virtues don't outweigh the flaws.

Black-and-White Characters:

- Fairy tale–like characters
- They're either good or bad
- The good tend to have little to no flaws
- The bad tend to have little to no virtues

Morally Gray Characters:

- A realistic take on characters
- There is generally no pure good or pure evil
- Every "good" character has a bad side to them
- Every "bad" character has a good side (redeeming qualities)

BONUS TIP

To really make use of your character's personality, try to think of it as the very prime obstacle to your character's goal.

What does this mean? If your character's goal is to defeat a horde of zombies coming to their small community, make them a coward. If your character's goal is to confidently win over the mysterious but beautiful new girl at their school, make them shy and awkward.

What does this do? It immediately creates a conflict within your character, and makes them act as their own biggest obstacle in the story. Good storytelling comes from contrast and conflict, and this is the first (and strongest) place you can implement that.

"The Airport Trick" for Character Diversity

Worried about your characters being too similar? There's a really neat and quick trick you can do to make sure this doesn't happen. Take each character from your cast and put them into the same situation (one that contains a problem or conflict for them), then write out their reaction. The goal is for each character to have a unique reaction to the problem.

For example: Your character is waiting at the airport gate to board their flight, and it's already two hours late. They go up to the attendant at the check-in counter and ask when the flight is going to leave. The attendant says if they had any updates, they would have announced them already. How does your character react?

Physical Description and Quirks

Now that you know the basics and have an image of your character in your mind, it's time to think about what they would look like on the page.

How do you go about writing physical descriptions? First of all, identifying your character as a blue-eyed brunette with pale skin isn't going to cut it. You want to be unique and intentional with your character's physicalities, and think about how these could actually build upon their personalities and who they are as a person, rather than having a simple visual shell for a character.

Major vs. Minor Characters. Minor characters should generally be more caricatured than your major ones. This helps us remember them and paint the image of them a lot quicker, since they're not going to have as much page time.

Physical description is an aspect that's difficult to nail down or explain, and it's very personal to every author's style, so I'll give you some interesting examples to look through when it comes to tackling this concretely in your prose.

The Presence Beats the Physicalities

Sometimes the physical descriptions don't matter as much as you might think. It's not the hair color that makes us connect to the character, but the way they carry themselves and the presence they have.

Mark Twain, *The Adventures of Huckleberry Finn*: "He was sunshine most always—I mean he made it seem like good weather."

F. Scott Fitzgerald, *The Great Gatsby*: "Her face was sad and lovely with bright things in it, bright eyes and a bright passionate mouth . . ."

Anne Brontë, *The Tenant of Wildfell Hall*: "His heart was like a sensitive plant, that opens for a moment in the sunshine, but curls up and shrinks into itself at the slightest touch of the finger, or the lightest breath of wind."

Incorporate physical descriptions into the theme of your book or your narrator's personality.

Joseph Conrad, *Heart of Darkness*: "He was commonplace in complexion, in features, in manners, and in voice. He was of middle size and of ordinary build. His eyes, of the usual blue, were perhaps remarkably cold, and he certainly could make his glance fall on one as trenchant and heavy as an axe. . . . Otherwise there was only an indefinable, faint expression of his lips, something stealthy—a smile—not a smile—I remember it, but I can't explain."

Notice how the author makes use of his character's voice in the description of someone he'd met.

Dennis Lehane, *A Drink Before the War*: "Sterling Mulkern was a florid, beefy man, the kind who carried weight like a weapon, not a liability. He had a shock of stiff white hair you could land a DC-10 on and a handshake that stopped just short of inducing paralysis."

Notice how Dennis Lehane uses the theme of war present in his book to describe the character.

Metaphors and Abstractions

This is my favorite way of thinking up descriptions for characters. Make them grotesque; compare them to abstract things that give the reader more of an emotion to go by, rather than a visual description.

Brian Morton, *Breakable You*: "Without her glasses Vivian did look a little frightening. She had tight sinewy strappy muscles and a face that was hardened and almost brutal—a face that might have been chiseled by a sculptor who had fallen out of love with the idea of beauty."

Fredrik Backman, *A Man Called Ove*: "People said Ove saw the world in black and white. But she was color. All the color he had."

Sherman Alexie, *The Lone Ranger and Tonto Fistfight in Heaven*: "I thought she was so beautiful. I figured she was the kind of woman who could make buffalo walk on up to her and give up their lives. She wouldn't have needed to hunt. Every time we went walking, birds would follow us around. Hell, tumbleweeds would follow us around."

Connect descriptions to their personality or their story.

For example, say you're writing about a woman who works as a baker. Use the setting of the bakery and the theme of sweetness to play into your character's description.

Instead of "She had a lovely bright smile reserved for each of her customers," try "Her smile was so sugary and sweet that her customers might have thought to complain over toothaches before even tasting the cupcakes she kept on display."

Rudyard Kipling, *The Jungle Book*: "A black shadow dropped down into the circle. It was Bagheera the Black Panther, inky black all over, but with the panther markings showing up in certain lights like the pattern of watered silk. Everybody knew Bagheera, and nobody cared to cross his path, for he was as cunning as Tabaqui, as bold as the wild buffalo, and as reckless as the wounded elephant. But he had a voice as soft as wild honey dripping from a tree, and a skin softer than down."

Notice how the author compares the panther to things found in the jungle (the setting of this book).

Leave space for interpretation.

Remember that it's OK to let your readers paint their own picture of a character. Going into too much detail can easily turn them off from the character altogether. This is where it's important to let go of the mindset that your character needs to look a certain way. You need to come to terms with the fact that no matter how well you describe your character, nobody is going to envision them the same way you do. So give your readers the foundations, and let them build the rest of the character in their own mind.

Internal vs. External Goals

Each of your major characters should have two goals: an internal and an external goal. The biggest difference between the two is that the internal goal is a **character-driving goal**, while the external is a **plot-driving goal**. This means the internal goal will be the one responsible for pushing your character journey forward and allowing for character development, while the external goal will be responsible for keeping the cogs of your plot moving forward and giving your characters something to chase.

Internal goal: An internal goal is a subconscious "goal" that lives inside a fictional character throughout the entirety of the story. This is a goal they are typically unaware of, and they have *no desire* to fulfill it. The internal goal is taken directly from your character's biggest flaw or struggle. When we meet them in the very first chapter of your novel, we'll immediately be aware of the flaws in their life, and we can assume these are things they will resolve by the end of the book.

Therefore, your **internal goal should be present from the very beginning of your novel**. What is something that's holding your character back from flourishing? What is that thing they've been ignoring or that thing they should have dealt with already? What is the flaw that's making their life more difficult?

Internal goals are referred to as **needs** for two reasons:

- They are *necessary* for a character to fulfill their character journey.
- The character is unaware of them for most of the story, and therefore they are not something they want (a conscious goal), but something they *need* (subconscious).

Examples of internal goals:

- Overcoming a fear
- Learning how to care of one's mental health
- Learning to be more open and receptive to others' kindness
- Letting go of the past and moving on
- Letting go of old habits
- Finding confidence
- Finding independence
- Finding faith
- Learning to accept things for what they are
- Finding peace or balance within oneself

External goal: An external goal is a conscious goal the character accepts at the beginning of your story and continues to pursue. This is a goal they are well aware of, and it's what *pushes them onward throughout most of the plot*. It represents a thing they're chasing.

Your character's external goal will typically not be present from the beginning of your story. **The external goal is directly prompted by the inciting incident** of your novel, and your character only actively starts chasing it in your second act.

There is an opportunity in every story to introduce **a second external goal**, and this place is the midpoint. We'll cover the specifics of the midpoint in the next chapter, but for now, know that your secondary external goal will be much higher stakes than the one prompted by the inciting incident. So, if you already have a big goal in mind that will hold up the plot of your story, it might be worth coming up with a smaller external goal to get your character going first, and save your big one for the plot twist.

External goals are referred to as *wants* because they are conscious goals your character desires to achieve, but that they don't need to achieve.

Examples of external goals:

- Winning over the romantic interest
- Defeating or killing the villain
- Getting a promotion
- Obtaining a special object
- Getting money
- Completing a job or quest
- Saving the princess from the tower
- Capturing a criminal
- Gaining popularity
- Tracking down information
- Solving a crime
- Saving the world

As you can see, these external goals feel very concrete, and you've probably already thought of a few examples of books and films where you may have seen these. Put your internal and external goals at odds, and you've got your conflict.

Internal Conflict Formula

Internal conflict happens when you put your internal and external goals at odds with one another. Typically, a character doesn't realize their internal goal (meaning they are oblivious to what they need to change about themselves in order to grow), and this directly results in them failing to complete their external goal (usually in the second half of act two). They then have to realize their internal goal and overcome it in order to have to a second chance at completing their external goal.

Will their agoraphobia keep them from helping a neighbor across the street, or can they overcome the root of the cause and help their neighbor out of danger? Will their heavy drinking affect their ability to solve a gruesome crime, or can they find the missing puzzle piece once sober? Will their insecurity keep them from finding true love, or will they finally accept their own flaws and confidently win over their love interest?

Here are some examples of internal conflict in popular fiction:

MEAN GIRLS (2004 FILM)

Cady's internal goal is to learn how to be true to herself. Her first external goal is to spy on the Plastics and ruin Regina. Her second external goal is to win over Aaron, her love interest. Her midpoint goal comes when she loses herself and realizes she is now the Queen Bee, and therefore her midpoint-prompted goal is to take over Regina's title completely.

Cady's mathlete team (which she ignores and quits while pursuing her external goals) is a **plot device** that actually portrays her internal goal—being true to herself. And when she rejoins them and wins the mathlete competition in the end, it's symbolic of her achieving her internal goal.

Internal conflict: Cady loses herself in the Plastics because of her tendency to adapt her personality. Because she's not being true to herself, she loses her true friends, then Aaron and even her spot in the Plastics. Once she realizes that she needs to be true to herself, she gets her friends back and completes the external goal of winning Aaron over.

TITANIC (1997 FILM)

Rose's internal goal is to break away from the aristocratic norms of her family and find her freedom. Her external goal is to be with Jack.

Internal conflict: Rose spends most of the film treading carefully and hiding from her family and her fiancé, and sneaking around with Jack, because she isn't ready to fight for her freedom. She achieves her internal goal at the very end of the film when she changes her name and flees from the family; however, her external goal remains incomplete.

THE HUNGER GAMES (BOOK BY SUZANNE COLLINS)

Katniss's internal goal is to be true to her own feelings. Her external goal is to survive the Hunger Games.

Internal conflict: She completes her external goal and survives the Hunger Games, but does so by pretending she has feelings for Peeta; therefore, she does not complete the internal goal. She becomes aware of her internal goal during the sequels but is forced into pretending and not being true to her feelings.

ROMEO AND JULIET (PLAY BY WILLIAM SHAKESPEARE)

Romeo and Juliet's internal goals were to find peace between their families or to find their own freedom. Their external goals were to be with each other.

Internal conflict: Romeo and Juliet failed their internal goal and, therefore, their external one as well.

From these examples, you can conclude that:

- A character doesn't necessarily have to complete either of their goals. This type of story is referred to as a tragedy.
- They typically need to complete their internal goal, and only then are they finally able to tackle the external one.
- They can complete their internal goal without proceeding to complete the external goal (either because it is no longer possible, or they've decided against it now that they know better).
- They can complete their external goal and become aware of their internal one, but be unable to do anything about it (causing a bittersweet ending).

Character Journey vs. Character Purpose

What is it? Character journey covers the change your character goes through from the beginning of the story to the end. Specifically, it follows your character becoming aware of their internal goal. Once you've figured out their internal conflict, you only need to place this within the context of your story and expand on it in order to write down your character journey.

To write up your character journey, think of:

Their starting point. What are they missing? What is their constriction? What is their flaw?

Their external goal that pushes them into action. What does the inciting incident prompt them to do?

Their realization of the internal goal. At what point do they realize they have to change, and what makes them see this?

Their completion of the internal goal, characterized by growth or change. Do they actually accept this realization and decide to do something about it? How?

Their final decision over their external goal. Do they tackle it again successfully? Do they change it? Do they leave it incomplete?

Remember, if you're writing a negative arc or your character never completes their internal goal, you should also adapt their journey to reflect this.

Having a character journey for all your most important characters will ultimately help you with rounding out your plot.

Purpose (Minor Characters)

One thing you will notice is different on your sheets for major and minor characters (pages 77-79) is that minor characters simply have a "purpose" where major ones have an internal conflict.

As I mentioned before, the purpose of your minor characters must be present, and it should be one of the following:

- To support your major character(s)
- To change your major character(s)
- To hinder your major character(s)

To Support

These characters will tend to be mentor figures or friends. They will usually feel balanced and complete, and they will tend to know more about life than your major character does.

How can they support your major character(s)?

- Point them in the right direction
- Teach them something
- Point out the things they're doing wrong
- Inspire them with their own work (or their words)

To Change

These characters will tend to be very different from the major character they are influencing. They usually have a very different view on life from your major character.

How can they change your major character(s)?

- Teach them something they didn't previously know
- Show them different ways of doing things
- Give them a different perspective on a problem
- Do something that changes the course of the major character(s)'s journey

In terms of the purpose of these characters, it might also be a less deliberate way of changing your character's story. Meaning it could be more plot related. For example, they might be put in danger or get kidnapped.

To Hinder

These characters will usually present an obstacle for your major characters. They might do it on purpose or subconsciously.

How can they hinder your major character(s)?

- Be a problem or someone they need to take care of (for example, an alcoholic or abusive parent)
- Be competitive with your major character and not want them to succeed
- Bully your major character
- Undermine them or betray their trust
- Use them for their own benefit

If you cannot appoint a single one of these purposes to a minor character in your story, then they are not a necessary character.

Character Backstories

You might have heard a lot about the significance of having a backstory for each of your characters, even if you won't end up including them in your project whatsoever. So does that mean you should craft a backstory for every single character you create? God no. Don't do that. Unless your project resembles the story structure of the 2004 TV series *Lost*. Then, by all means.

Crafting a character backstory can help you get to know your character better. You've probably heard this before. And yes, it's very true that knowing where your character came from and how they came to be in the situation you're now putting them in can be a major help to clarifying your story line, your character motivations and the reasoning behind their goals.

But you don't need to know every detail of each of your character's lives in order to know them, so don't slip down a slope of crafting intricate histories for all your major characters if you don't need one. This is one of those stages where a lot of writers get too stuck in the planning of their characters and never actually get to writing them. Proceed with caution!

Ultimately, whatever backstory you come up with, most of it won't make it into your final draft, but it will help round out your characters and make them feel more realistic, even if you merely hint at their past. Just because you crafted out their backstories doesn't mean you must include them in your draft as such. Here are the situations where you *shouldn't* fall back on the crutch of backstory:

You're not exploring anything new about the character.

- We already knew about the character traits you showcase in the backstory, from the present timeline.
- You're using it as an info dump.
- It's forced into the story to gain sympathy for the character.
- It's an obvious afterthought and doesn't feel natural to the plot.

Here are the situations where your backstory can actually be useful to the reader:

- We discover a new part of the character's personality.
- It fits into your present-time plot (it's not an afterthought but an actual part of the story).
- It directly affects the character's actions in your current plot.

Exploring your characters' backstories should be used to find out where their flaw or misbelief came from. The backstory should be the reason as to why your character finds themselves in that equilibrium of your story.

The Character Tree Method

Making characters is an exciting process. For some writers, it's so exciting that they end up with far too many characters and no story to place them into. The best way to avoid this is to start with your protagonist and work your way out. Make sure you have fully developed your protagonist, and that you have at least a vague idea of your story, before you go crazy with thinking up a massive cast of characters. More often than not, you'll need a lot less characters than you think you will.

Knowing Whether Your Character Is Relevant

To spare yourself hours of torture in figuring out whether your character actually contributes to the story, ask yourself one very simple question: **Does this character have any relation to my protagonist(s)?** If the answer is no, that character has no place in your manuscript!

Another case where your character may be irrelevant is if they have the same purpose as another. If you have two characters whose purpose in the story is to teach your protagonist an important lesson (particularly if it's the same lesson), ask yourself whether they're both needed, or whether you could merge them into a single character to carry that same purpose.

The Character Tree Method

This method is a great way to make sure each of the characters in your story has some sort of connection to the protagonist. Start with putting your hero in the center of the tree. Around them, place everyone who is closely related or connected to them through plot significance or relationships, such as:

- The antagonist
- The best friend(s)
- The love interest
- The teacher/mentor
- The family, parents/parent figures

This is your **first line of connections**.

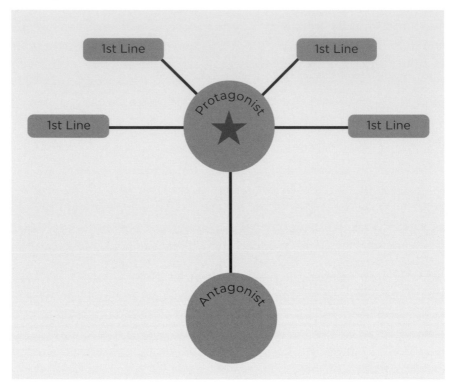

Once you have your protagonist's closest relationships in the tree, check where the rest of your characters fit into. This could be:

- The best friend's parents
- The love interest's best friend
- The best friend's love interest
- The villain's right hand
- The extended familial relationships

These characters compose your second line of connections.

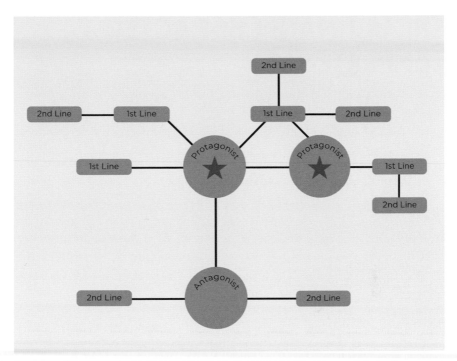

If there is any character you have put on the tree who does not connect to the protagonist or any of the protagonist's first line of connections, this character is likely irrelevant to the plot.

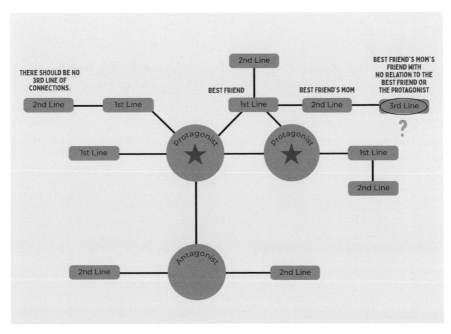

THE ULTIMATE CHARACTER TEMPLATE

Here's a quick look at the templates I use with all my writing clients and for my own projects as well. They will cover all the major points we discussed in this chapter, and you can use them as a guideline to crafting your characters.

Keep in mind, you might discover new characters as you start working on your book, so you can always come to this section and craft a new sheet for characters as you introduce them. For a lot of writers, it's much easier to have a very general idea of who their characters are, and discover more about them as they actually sit down to write them. This is totally normal! Figure out a way that works for you, and fill these out as needed.

Sometimes you might find yourself stuck in a scene with a specific character, and nine times out of ten, the reason will be that you haven't given them enough off-page work. So, take a step back, return to these templates and see if you can find out more about them.

Now you should be able to craft layered, complex characters and use these templates to make sure you've covered all the biggest aspects.

If you get stuck during your writing process, the best idea is to revisit these templates, and see whether there might have been something you missed. Most writing issues actually come from not knowing characters well enough, which is why I've prepared some exercises you can follow in the next section with the specific intent of getting to know your characters better.

MAJOR CHARACTER SHEET

Name:

Story Role:

Traits & Quirks

Personality

Flaws _____

Virtues _____

Voice

Phrases _____

External Goal

+

Internal Goal

↓

Internal Conflict

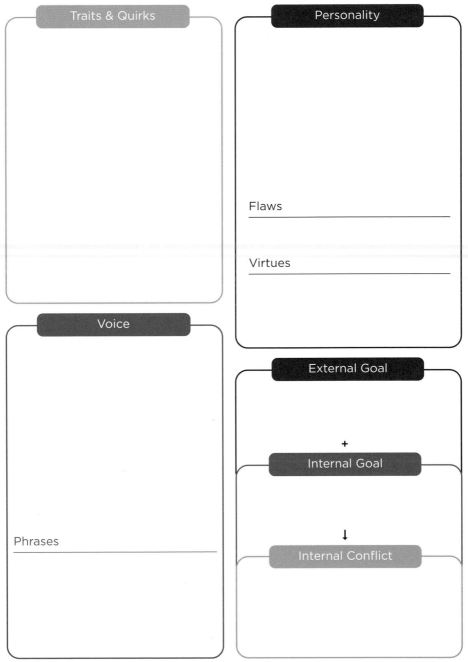

Journey

Equilibrium

Disequilibrium

New Equilibrium

Backstory

MINOR CHARACTER SHEET

Name:

Story Role:

Traits & Quirks

Personality

Flaws _____

Virtues _____

Voice

Phrases _____

Story Purpose

CHARACTER EXERCISES

⭐ Write a letter from a character whose voice you're struggling to nail down. Have them talk about something that excites them, something they hate and something that makes them uncomfortable.

⭐ Put your character into their worst nightmare, and write a short story about it. How do they react? Is it a fight, flight or freeze response? If someone they love is endangered in this scenario, what will they do?

⭐ Explore a childhood memory connected to a specific object which your character has in their possession at the time of your story. Write it as a short piece of self-contained fiction.

⭐ What is your character's secret? Something they don't want anyone to know about them? Put them in a situation where this is very close to coming out, and explore their reaction by writing out the scene.

⭐ Write an email, a blog post or a letter from your character's point of view, but set it ten years after the events of your story. Where are they now? What has changed? Who are they writing to, and who are they writing about?

⭐ Imagine your character is forced to clean out their space and pack their things up. When writing this, think about what sort of objects they come across, and what these mean to them. Which ones can they throw out willy-nilly, and which ones do they linger on? Which ones do they choose to keep, and why?

⭐ If your character had the opportunity to orchestrate their own death and plan their own funeral knowing they had to die that day, what would that look like? Would they go out in style? Would they favor a painless approach over a memorable exit? What final song would they pick? Who would they invite to the funeral? And who would they spend their last day with? Would they ask anyone to help them?

- What is your character's biggest regret? Something they would rush back to fix without hesitation? Write out their memory of this moment and exactly what they would have done differently

- Your character comes home late after a really busy day and they're starving. They go to the fridge and open it. What do they see inside, and what can this tell you about their personality?

- Your character is forced to make a really important speech at school or work or in front of a large community of people. Write the speech as they would prepare it. Bonus: Write the scene of them actually delivering the speech!

- Your character is attending a class in which a professional educator speaks about a topic that your character knows inside and out, but the educator clearly doesn't. What is your characters thought process? Do they speak up? Do they ask questions? Do they quietly stew?

- Your character is in a small local grocery store during a robbery. In the store are also an elderly person, a child and another adult. What does your character do, and how would this situation unfold?

HOW TO PLAN YOUR NOVEL

THE THREE-ACT STORY STRUCTURE

We've gotten to the scary part! Lots of writers dread planning out their novels, and it's often presented as a thing to be frowned upon. Planning sucks all the fun out of writing! I've heard this too many times to count.

But contrary to popular belief, I'm not here to make you pull up a detailed chapter-by-chapter treatment of every little thing that happens in your story. The approach I use is a very easy three-act structure that outlines the most important plot points of your story, but leaves more than enough room for creativity and changes. In fact, most of my clients' projects (and my own writing projects) have changed immensely from the first time they were planned out. This is totally natural and expected. Just because you lay out the bones of your story doesn't mean you're limiting yourself or your path for this narrative. You're simply laying down those foundations to keep yourself on track.

The structure I'll take you through is based on Todorov's theory of equilibrium, which we mentioned earlier (and which is why I encouraged you to get familiar with it before getting to this stage of plotting!). Act 1 is your equilibrium, act 2 is the disequilibrium and act 3 is the establishment of the new equilibrium. It also pulls elements from Blake Snyder's *Save the Cat!* Beat Sheet, and from the classic template of the hero's journey. From all of these, I've compiled a template I call the plot grid (page 85), which should work flexibly for most types of stories and genres (unless you're trying something really experimental).

The best thing about this template is that it's all laid out on one single page.

THE PLOT GRID TEMPLATE

The plot grid can be a scary thing to look at. But don't worry, it's actually really simple. It's split into four equal parts, and the general rule of thumb is that each of these parts should make up 25 percent of your story.

- **Act 1 (25 percent):** Serves as the setup to your story, where we get to know the characters and understand what they're going to have to deal with in this book.
- **Act 2 (50 percent):** Act 2 is split into two parts, the first one being more lighthearted with your character exploring the world and its obstacles, while the second is more serious and includes the point where things start to go very wrong.
- **Act 3 (25 percent):** The resolution to your story. This act should follow how your character(s) deal with all the mess, how (or if) they come out the other end and what they learn in the process.

The percentage split is a rule you don't need to stick too rigidly to; accept it as a guideline, but don't stress over it. The good news is that if you've followed along with the book so far, you've already done most of the work. Once you have your character journeys worked out, you have the most important parts.

Now, it's just down to organizing your plot and filling in the gaps.

ACT 1
The Setup
Chapters

ACT 2
The Adventure
Chapters

ACT 2
The Chaos
Chapters

ACT 3
The Resolution
Chapters

Setup
First Image
Story Question
Status Quo & Flaws

Inciting Incident
Inciting Incident

The Debate
Hesitation
Acceptance

New World
Ups and Downs
Midpoint

Things Go South
Punch in the Cut
Giving Up

Light Bulb
Finale
Final Image

ACT 1 - THE SETUP

Act 1 serves as your story's setup. Typically, this is where we'll find out:

- Who the hero is
- What sort of situation they're trapped in
- What they need to learn
- What their world looks like
- What sets their story in motion and pushes them out of their comfort zone
- How they deal with the inciting incident and what choice they make
- Which external goal they are chasing

We'll separate act 1 into three sections: Setup, Inciting Incident and Debate.

Setup

There are three parts to the setup:

- **First Image** - Our first look into the protagonist's world
- **Story Question** - A hint at the deeper message your book is tackling
- **Status Quo and Flaws** - Your protagonist's normal and everything that's wrong with it

Your setup should typically fit into your first two chapters.

First Image

The first image has one main purpose: to outline exactly who your character is before anything in your story happens to them. Why? Because you're going to want to connect your first image to your final image to show the journey your character went through, by comparing who they were (first image) to who they are now (final image). *It's all about highlighting that change.*

So, when you're thinking of what you want your first image to be, make sure you think about what the final one will look like, too. What does your character need to learn? What are they struggling with at the very beginning? How are they going to overcome this?

Story Question

The story question is not a strict plot point. But it gets its very own box in the plot grid because it is a key part of the story you shouldn't forget to establish.

We learned that the message of the story is typically drawn from your hero's need, from their flaw, from what they need to overcome. The story question simply builds on that. But how do you showcase your story question in the plot?

You can do it through any of the following:

- A line and/or sentence in narration (a character who will attempt to earn forgiveness for their sins might reveal to readers in the beginning that they don't ever expect to be forgiven)
- A piece of dialogue (a side character who subtly highlights what the protagonist needs to learn)
- A small physical event that acts as a metaphor for what the character needs to overcome (for example, we might meet a character who struggles to gain trust of a wild horse, but their journey will be to learn how to gain trust as a leader of their people)

Your themes and your story question should generally appear in the first chapter or two. The quicker you establish them, the easier it will be for your reader to pick up on why they should care about your story. Just make sure your hint at the story question is not obvious or forced into the story.

Status Quo and Flaws

The status quo is your protagonist's normal "comfortable" day-to-day life. It's what they're used to. But this routine should always have flaws or struggles. The flaws highlight everything within their normal that is uncomfortable, unbalanced or just wrong. These flaws are then what we expect the character to expel from their life by the end of the story.

In *The Seven Husbands of Evelyn Hugo* by Taylor Jenkins Reid, we meet the narrator Monique Grant. What we learn about her status quo is that she works for *Vivant* magazine and lives alone in a small apartment. What we learn about her flaws is that she's underappreciated at work, that she fails to stand up for herself and that she's undergoing a messy divorce—these are all the things we expect to be changed or resolved by the end of the book.

Inciting Incident

The inciting incident is the event that sets your story in motion. It's the event that breaks your character's status quo. It thrusts them into action, and it makes them do something out of the ordinary for them.

- Monique Grant gets chosen to do an interview with Evelyn Hugo.
- Bilbo Baggins receives a party of dwarves at Bag End.
- Peter Parker gets bitten by a spider.

The inciting incident changes everything and pulls your character out of the comfortable and into the unknown.

The Debate

The debating section is split into two parts.

Hesitation - Your hero takes some time to think about the inciting incident and process what it means. They might weigh their options for a while and remain undecided on their next steps. They might even entirely refuse their call-to-action and walk away.

Acceptance - This is the point where your hero makes the conscious decision to act on the inciting incident, to head out on the adventure and do something about it. The acceptance might be prompted by urgency, or by adding an extra stake into the equation. For example, if they refused the call-to-action at first, then they might get an extra shove in that direction, where they're forced to accept.

Once you've set up your story, and your hero has decided to do something about it, you can break into act 2.

Act 2 is divided into two parts: The Adventure and The Chaos

ACT 2 - THE ADVENTURE

The Adventure is the first, lighter part of act 2.

It's divided into:

- New World
- Ups and Downs
- Midpoint

New World

The New World is where your real story actually begins. This is usually defined by:

- A new location where your story will be set
- A new cast of characters
- An overall unfamiliar situation for your character

New World is all about **novelty** for your character. You're setting up a world they are unfamiliar with but have now accepted to enter into. It doesn't have to be an entirely new world, but it will be the first glimpse of the new situation in which they find themselves.

The New World is a good place to give the first test to your character. You can outline a quest for them or present them with the first actionable step toward their external goal. Keep in mind, we're at the start of your character's story, so whatever test you give them, they may not be successful at it. You want to keep with the realism here that they need to grow and learn in order to actually do things right.

This is also a great place to start a secondary plotline, like a secondary main character, a secondary narrator or simply the beginning of a subplot.

Ups and Downs

Ups and Downs are usually an open playing field. Think of it as an obstacle course your hero is taking for the first time. While they run through it, they might discover:

- New things about the world
- New bonds and relationships
- New challenges to tackle
- More information about their external goal

But they will also, more than likely, be held back by **their ignorance of their internal goal**.

The Ups and Downs is like an explorative journey filled with interesting but harmless obstacles. These are the obstacles your character can bounce back from and learn from. The Ups and Downs is also a great part of the story to hint at your **antagonistic forces**. This means that you should think of potentially implementing a warning to your protagonist of how things might go wrong, or how the antagonist could gain an upper hand, or how this goal they're chasing shouldn't be their primary focus. At this point, your protagonist will likely dismiss this, or they won't even be aware of the extent of the danger in the first place. But including this hint will make your next act feel a lot more planned and sensible.

Midpoint

The midpoint, also known as the turning point, is the first moment in your story that something substantial happens on your character's way to reaching their external goal. The midpoint might also change the direction of their story.

It can be:

A False Victory - Your hero completes an important milestone toward their goal, and they gain a false sense of confidence. Their ego grows, and they think they have it all figured out. This will make them fall much harder when they hit The Chaos.

A Plot Twist - Your hero discovers a new piece of information that changes the course they're taking. Maybe what they set out to achieve wasn't the real goal. Maybe they've discovered a new threat. In either case, this significantly changes your character's plan.

Whichever way you roll the dice, the midpoint should be introducing a brand new piece of information into the mix, something your character was not previously aware of or able to achieve.

The midpoint is also a great place to introduce a secondary external goal for your character. If you remember, our first external goal was prompted by the inciting incident, and it was the goal we've been rooting to achieve since then. Now is your chance to flip the story around and introduce a new goal, which now seems way more important than the one you led the story with.

ACT 2 - THE CHAOS
The Chaos is where everything falls apart. This is the doom and gloom portion of your story. We're going to separate it into:

- Things Go South
- Punch in the Gut
- Giving Up

Things Go South
At this point your antagonistic forces start to gain the upper hand on your hero. Now, keep in mind that if you're writing a story where there are no personified villains, this still works the same way. Your antagonistic forces can be:

- Your character themselves (self-sabotage)
- Society or circumstance
- Natural disasters
- Any other nonphysical antagonistic force

For Things Go South, you have three boxes. As a general guideline, I like to separate three different events, or three different things to fall apart or go wrong for your hero, before the Punch in the Gut moment. It can also be two to three different stages of one bad situation. The idea behind this is to build up momentum so that every little thing your hero has worked to build up starts to crumble, one by one. They're hit with many things, one right after the other, and they struggle to keep up.

Punch in the Gut

Once all the bad things pile up and your hero thinks it can't get any worse, you hit them with a massive Punch in the Gut. You take away the one thing they always thought they could count on. The one thing that was always there for them. The one thing they never thought they would lose.

The Punch in the Gut moment works best if it's unexpected. For example:

- An innocent's death (a pet, a child, a happy-go-lucky supportive character)
- A betrayal by a close friend (someone who's been there all along turning their back on your hero)
- The loss of an object (one with a special emotional connection to your protagonist)

What the Punch in the Gut moment needs to do is deliver the very final blow to kick your hero down. It can be a very tiny thing, too, if you wish. Think of it as the proverbial straw that broke the camel's back. The kick in the toe after a horrible day.

Giving Up

Giving Up is the grieving process your hero must go through after everything has been taken from them. This is where your hero might:

- Lose all hope
- Give up
- Refuse to fight anymore
- Retreat to their old ways
- Cut the remainder of their ties

Depending on your story, this part can happen really quickly, through just one scene, or you might even draw it out into several chapters. You could allow your protagonist to physically return to the place where we first met them, before they embarked on their adventure. But this time, after everything they've been through, they will be acutely aware of the drawbacks of this situation, and it will feel even worse than when they first accepted their call-to-action. Why? Because now they know what they could have had if they'd just kept fighting for it.

ACT 3 - THE RESOLUTION
Act 3 is split into:

- Light Bulb
- Finale
- Final Image

This is probably the easiest to figure out, if you've set up all your building blocks right. If you have paid special attention to being specific in your Things Go South blocks, this is going to be a piece of cake.

Light Bulb
We left off with your hero in a pit of grueling misery and self-pity. Now we have to snap them out of it. This is where the whole idea of your book comes together, and you could consider this the most important moment of your novel. It's where the hero experiences the internal realization and becomes who they were meant to be. They learn a crucial message of the story and experience the internal change.

How can you do this?

- Use a minor, seemingly unimportant character (share something inspiring with them, change their point of view)
- Use a meaningful object (reminds them what they're fighting for)
- Use a line they've heard before, but now means so much more (again, something that sparks their inner purpose and gives them new hope)

One of my favorite aha-moments in media is in the film *The Secret Life of Walter Mitty*:

Walter has a boring office job, and a mother who keeps all of his trinkets since childhood, reminding him of how adventurous he used to be. He then sets out on his own adventure around the world. During a low point, Walter disposes of a wallet he received as a gift on his adventures. He tosses it in the trash. Turns out, there was an important piece of camera roll in the wallet, which costs him his job. He gives up, he focuses on "real life," his family, the simplicity of it all. And just when he's decided that everything is over and done with and he should move on, he sees the wallet at his mom's. "I always save your trinkets," she says. And to top it off, the wallet is engraved with an inspirational quote, which gives Walter the hope he needed.

This uses all three tricks I mentioned above:

- A minor, seemingly unimportant character, who's always been there
- A meaningful object
- A line both they and we have heard before, which now means so much more than it did the first time

Other examples of characters finally coming to terms with their internal conflict and changing their viewpoints can be found in numerous works of fiction, such as:

In Matt Haig's *The Midnight Library*, Nora finally realizes that all the lives she's been trying to live weren't her own, and she needed to come to the realization that she doesn't actually want to die, which also answers the biggest question of the book.

In Mary Shelley's *Frankenstein*, when the scientist finally realizes the mistake he's made by creating and abandoning his monster, he knows it's too late to fix it.

When Rapunzel from Disney's *Tangled* recognizes the symbol of her kingdom that she's been subconsciously drawing for years, she realizes she's the lost princess.

When Katniss Everdeen from *The Hunger Games* decides not to allow the Capitol the control she's been under the entire book, and uses poisonous berries to threaten the entire system, she simultaneously comes to terms with her own mortality and freedom of choice.

Finale

The finale is where you wrap up all your loose ends. Your hero sets out on their mission once again, but this time with a changed perspective and a different approach. They've learned, they've changed, they're no longer that person we met in act 1—they are visibly different. And now they have true confidence to act on. They tackle their issues one by one, with a much higher success rate than before.

This is where you can go back to your Things Go South, determine everything that went wrong for them and decide how they tackle each problem. They don't necessarily have to be successful at each of the things that fell apart earlier; some things they might not ever be able to get back, such as the death of an important character, but they can definitely remember the moment or use it as motivation.

Final Image

We've already touched on the Final Image when we spoke about the First Image during act 1 and how these two connect. Let's remind ourselves how to pull this off. The idea of the Final Image is that it draws a parallel between who your character started out as during the First Image versus who they are now in the Final Image. It is meant to portray the change and the growth that your hero went through.

Consider drawing a parallel between one of these things:

- The same physical location
- The same situation
- The same surrounding characters

Place your hero in the exact same (or a similar) situation at the beginning and the end of your book, and make sure you're able to showcase the change they went through and how they're better off now because of it.

SUBPLOTS

We hear a lot about subplots, about their importance and how you should have many of them in your book. First of all, this varies by genre. Some genres are typically a lot bulkier than others. They might, therefore, have more characters and more plotlines.

Technically, you can tell one main story line following this plot grid without having to add any more subplots, and it will still work as a story.

What are subplots? Subplots are plot threads that can be woven through the story to further support or strengthen your main plot. They typically involve secondary characters.

What is their purpose? The purpose of subplots is to draw a more realistic view of your world. They flesh out the rest of your characters and give them a place in your story. They can also raise the stakes, add depth to your main story line and introduce more conflict.

What can they do specifically?

- **Raise the stakes or increase the urgency.** Something unexpected happens that rushes your protagonist or changes their plan—someone they care about follows them into battle—adding a distraction and a risk.
- **Expand on your supporting characters.** What is the hero's best friend struggling with? They might have an ongoing fight with their parents that later results in them being kicked out, having to seek help from your hero.
- **Serve a betrayal.** Someone they were close to is working behind their back and later teams up with the antagonist.
- **Add depth to relationships.** In more plot-driven books, the romance might often be a subplot and treated as such.

Any subplot you think of should impact your main plot one way or another.

You can craft any number of subplots throughout your novel, and the easiest way to do so is to pick the major characters who will lead each of the subplot threads. If you have already outlined their character journey, you should have the subplot ready, and now all you have to do is find a space for it in your plot grid.

Your subplots don't necessarily have to follow the exact structure of your main story line. This means that your secondary character's Punch in the Gut moment doesn't necessarily need to happen at the exact same time your protagonist's does, but do make sure they are following the main story line at a reasonable proximity. For example, the secondary character's Punch in the Gut could happen during the main story line's Things Go South, but it really shouldn't happen during the main story line's Debate.

ALL ABOUT CHAPTERS

DETERMINING THE CHAPTERS

You'll notice that your plot grid has a space for determining your chapters based on your plot points, right there on the one page. So, how do you go about this? How do you know what should be a chapter, and what should be the next chapter and then a chapter after that?

What actually needs to go into a chapter?

Basically, your chapter has to have a point. However, contrary to popular belief, not every chapter needs to cover a plot point. Your chapter should build on one or more of the following:

- Plot
- Character
- Relationships
- Theme
- World-building

As long as your chapter advances or changes any of the mentioned elements, it's likely there for a reason, and you don't need to force any extra plot points into it.

CHAPTER LENGTH, TITLES AND DEVICES

First of all, let's make sure you understand one thing. **Your chapter doesn't need to be any certain length.** Your chapters also don't need to be the same length overall. This is one of the most common questions I get asked by my clients, especially first-time writers, and it's an important thing to note. It's more than OK to have shorter chapters and longer ones. It's completely up to you to determine what feels right. Some authors don't even use chapters at all.

Know the difference between scenes and chapters.

A scene is usually tied to a certain location and time. These are little fragments commonly used in plays and movies, but they can be handy to consider in novels, too. As novel writing is a more free-flowing medium where the writer has complete control over narrative time, separating scenes isn't always necessary. You can use transitional paragraphs which talk about the passage of time and what your characters got up to in that time, and this is perfectly acceptable as long as it's entertaining and purposeful in the story.

But you might want to include scenes, too. Simply end one and crash straight into another one, without transitioning your readers from one place to another. You can think of this as a cut in a film. One moment we're with your hero at a family dinner, and the very next they're back in the car with their spouse, driving home.

These little fragments are scenes, and several scenes can form a longer chapter.

Devices

Another thing you can use in your novel are different devices to tell your story. These are things like:

- Letters
- Journal entries
- Emails
- Crime scene documents
- Blog posts
- Text messages
- Audio recording transcriptions
- Poems or plays
- Recipes
- Legends

These can make your book feel more interactive and help break up the prose. You can also tell a story entirely through devices; the most classic example of this is Bram Stoker's *Dracula*, written through a series of letters and journal entries.

Not every book will need a device, but it can be helpful in some cases. Something to consider when choosing the narrative perspective of your novel.

Think of devices as techniques to add more mystery to your story, or deliver information in a way that positions your readers as detectives. This doesn't necessarily have to be exclusive to the crime genre (although it works very well if you want to give your readers a first-hand look into the clues that your character may be gathering, such as transcripts, recordings, articles, etc.), but it can also be beneficial in other genres to create a sub-narrative, such as including small legends in fantasy novels which build on the story world and give extra context to your story (as in *The Fifth Season* by N. K. Jemisin); or perhaps snippets of blogs and online commentary which can paint a picture of your character's struggle with their online presence (as in *The Seven Husbands of Evelyn Hugo* by Taylor Jenkins Reid); or snippets of old recipes and vintage magazine publications to further reinforce the theme of your story (as in *Recipe for a Perfect Wife* by Karma Brown).

Devices, just like any other part of a novel, should be chosen for a valid reason, whether this is to expand on the world you're building, deliver your story in the context of "found diaries," or reinforce the thematic architecture of your novel.

CHAPTER STRUCTURE

Some of the most common questions I receive as a coach are: "How am I supposed to structure my chapter?" "Is there a template I can use?" "Is there a preferred length?" And if you're wondering the same thing, know it's OK, because there seems to be no straightforward information anywhere on how a chapter should be structured. On the one hand, how you structure your chapters is up to you. You can be creative with this, and most of the time it's based on what *feels* right. You should be able to tell whether your chapter is structured well or not, the more you write and the more you read.

But if you're one of those people who need a clear pointer for this, I've got you. We'll do this in steps.

Step #1: Determine what your chapter builds on. Is it plot, character, relationships, theme, world or a mixture?

Step #2: Determine the most important plot point of your chapter. What is the *one main thing* this chapter is actually about? Again, the plot point can also refer to an important step in a relationship (especially if you're writing literary or romance fiction).

Step #3: Determine the journey of this chapter. The one thing a chapter must do is to show some kind of change. Whatever kind of situation you open your chapter with needs to somehow transform by the end of it. It can happen in one of three ways:

- Progress
- Regress
- Change

Typically the only time a chapter will feel pointless and redundant is when it doesn't do any of these things. If everything still feels the same at the end of the chapter as it did at the beginning, then what is the point?

Step #4: Write a few sentences that highlight that journey.

To do this, you can use a small version of the equilibrium method, but adapt it to that main point you're tackling.

- Equilibrium - the starting point and your character's current situation
- Disequilibrium - something out of the ordinary happens that changes things, makes your character uncomfortable, or puts them in a conflicting or difficult position
- New equilibrium - how the situation or the character has changed

For example, at the beginning of your chapter, your character is sulking about an unsuccessful quest they've just come back from. This is your equilibrium. Next, another character comes to join them and pushes them into a situation where they have to open up and talk about their failure. Your character refuses, so their friend tells them a story about when they found themselves in a similar situation. Your character would rather be anywhere else. This is your disequilibrium. Finally, the friend makes a point. Despite their best efforts, your character gets really into the story, and they learn new information about their friend that they weren't previously aware of. This changes: 1) their outlook on things and 2) their feelings toward their friend. This is your new equilibrium.

Step #5: Use the ultimate "show don't tell" trick. Once you have the main journey of the chapter worked out it might be helpful to break it down into beats. Beats are little important sections of your story that you want to touch on. Think of them as a simple bullet-point outline for everything you want to happen in your chapters.

I like to combine this beat sheet with a game that challenges my "show don't tell" abilities. It works in two ways:

- Allows you to get creative with showing instead of telling
- Helps you bulk out your chapters

It's super easy, and you can do it by creating a very simple, very basic chapter plan.

- Write down a bullet-point list of all the things you need your reader to know after reading this chapter. Make sure that this list is as concise and to-the-point as possible.
- Tackle each point by challenging yourself to never use any of the words you used to explain your bullet point to yourself. You can do this by inventing a situation to showcase the bullet point in a more natural way. For example, if you want to show your character as indecisive, put them in a situation where they're forced to make a decision, and never let yourself use the word "indecisive" or "decision." If you want to show your character has a good work ethic, invent a situation where their coworker goes home sick and your character picks up their workload.

HOW TO
ACTUALLY WRITE
YOUR NOVEL

TACKLING THE FIRST DRAFT

This is where things get real.

Now, it's no secret that what writers struggle with the most is actually sitting down to write. Outlining and planning things in your head is all good and well, but writing the thing down? It can feel like an impossible task.

Before we jump into this, I want you to know that it's totally normal to feel super overwhelmed by the idea of writing this project down. On average, a novel will be at least 80,000 words long, and that's not easy to achieve. Writing a book is difficult! Anyone who tells you it's easy probably isn't doing it right, or they might be an alien. Or Stephen King. Either way, not a comparable entity! So, allow yourself to feel a little scared by this task. It's what makes writing exciting after all. If you can finish this book, you can do anything you set your mind to.

If you're a newbie writer or you just need some advice on how to approach the actual technical word-for-word writing of a novel, we are going to explore just that in this chapter.

NARRATIVE PERSPECTIVE

OK, so you've got your idea, you've got your characters, the plot is worked out and you're ready to go. But who's going to tell the story?

This is where your **narrator** comes in.

There are lots of different types of narrators you could have in your story, and you could experiment with different perspectives or different approaches to narrating this.

Finding the correct narrative position is absolutely crucial to your story, and is often something that gets ignored or decided as an afterthought. But if you take a second to study what different narrative perspectives you have available to you, you might find one that suits your story much better than one you had originally chosen.

What I want you to keep in mind as an author is that your narrator and your protagonist are two different entities and two different choices. Just because you've chosen a protagonist(s), it doesn't mean they automatically have to be the narrator as well.

First Person
I opened the door for him, forcing a smile as my hello.

You're probably already familiar with this perspective. It's the simplest one to master for a new writer, but it does come with its own challenges. For this perspective, you need to absolutely nail down the internal voice of your narrator. The first person perspective is told entirely through a character's own thoughts and actions. We see and feel everything they do, but we're limited in our knowledge beyond that one character. We only get access to that person's thoughts, and we know nothing about the other characters, unless we're told something about them that our narrator knows. The first person is the absolutely closest you can ever get to a character, and it's the best position for creating a significant connection between reader and narrator, making them almost one and the same.

Where it gets complicated is if you're looking to include multiple first person perspectives in your story. Oftentimes, this is done very poorly as the distinctions between character registers aren't significant enough to fully immerse your reader into both voices. There is also the question of your reader's suspension of disbelief, which is much harder to achieve through a first person narrator, let alone several. Logically, your readers will know all the characters are written by the same author, and therefore the immersion into several different characters' heads from such a close perspective becomes that much harder.

So, if you're looking to include several perspectives, think about whether using a third person focalized perspective might be more effective for you. With that, there is less strain on unique internal voices and a more natural flow between perspectives, as well as an easier approach to your reader's suspension of disbelief.

Second Person
You opened the door for him, forcing a smile as your hello.

This is a perspective that's not very commonly utilized in books but is more present in shorter pieces. It's quite difficult to tell an entire novel through a second person narrator, but it can be done. More often, it's used for a single perspective, or as an "interlude" between chapters. This is one you can get very creative with, because you're leading your reader by the hand into your world.

Second person can feel a lot like a game, and it has been used to create "choose your own story" types of novels, so if this is something you're interested in, this perspective might be the one for you.

If you want to see this perspective in action, and explore using several different narrative perspectives in one book, I'd highly recommend reading *The Fifth Season* by N. K. Jemisin and *Dragonfall* by L. R. Lam.

First Person Direct Address
I opened the door for you, forcing a smile as my hello.

Similarly to second person, this is a perspective that speaks directly to your reader, but the difference here is that there is a separate narrator they interact with. Think of it as having both a subject (the narrator) and an object (the reader) within your narrative, while in second person you're focusing on the object. Again, this is a less commonly used perspective in long-form narratives, but it's certainly something you can experiment with.

First Person Plural
We opened the door for him, forcing a smile as our hello.

An even rarer narrative form is the first person plural. Likely this is something you can use for only very specific narratives, such as having a narrator who's part of a cult, community or some utopian or dystopian organization, or perhaps a sci-fi/fantasy situation with several entities within one body! A really cool use of the first person plural can be found in *Bunny* by Mona Awad, where most of the story is told from a regular first person perspective, but transitions slowly into plural as the protagonist gets more and more absorbed into a cult.

Third Person Focalized
She opened the door for him, forcing a smile as her hello.

Third person focalized is actually the very same thing as first person perspective, but with the use of different pronouns. You can treat it the same way in terms of its rules, meaning your reader will only have access to the thoughts, feelings and perceptions of the character which your narrator is "focalized" onto. The pros of this perspective is that it's much easier to switch between characters without taking your readers out of the narrative, or testing their suspension of disbelief.

However, one thing to consider that not many writers do is that third person focalized should still have elements of your character's narrative voice in it. For example, if you're switching between a third focalized narrative of a nine-year-old and one of a twenty-year-old, the narrative voices you use for each of these should be different. With the nine-year-old, you might not use vocabulary that's too serious or advanced, and with the twenty-year-old, you might use terms or expressions that are popular among that age group. Either way, these narrative voices, even if not told directly from the characters themselves, should still filter their voices and personalities.

A common mistake to be aware of when writing third person focalized is **head-hopping**. Head-hopping is a jarring narrative approach where you start off with a focus on one character, sticking to what they're thinking and feeling, but then you switch to a different character in the middle of the scene. For example, your protagonist (and the person we are currently following) is speaking to their love interest, and suddenly we're told exactly how that love interest is feeling, and even what they're thinking. This can make your reader feel ungrounded, as they won't be sure whose story they're following.

Different Levels of Focalization

With third person focalized, you can also experiment with levels of focalization that you want to utilize. Are you going to be completely present in your character's head and let your readers hear their present-moment thoughts? Or will you only give little hints and insights into what that character might be feeling? If you think of your narrative device as a camera, try to imagine how closely that camera follows your character. Is it right by their ear, or a couple steps behind them?

The level of focalization is something you should try to keep consistent within your narrative, too. We don't want to get used to a narrator that holds back, only to suddenly be thrust into the head of the character we're following, unless this is done purposefully.

Third Person Detached

She opened the door for him with a smile that appeared ingenuine.

This detached type of narrator is one you can think of as a simple **observer**. Like a stalker in the bushes who's following your characters around and then telling readers everything they see. The important thing about this narrator that you should be aware of is that they will have very limited information. This narrator will be kept **entirely out of your characters' heads** and can only assume what they're feeling or thinking, but can never say so for certain.

Third Person Omniscient

She opened the door for him, but the missus was well-known for faking her smiles to strangers, so Larry could have assumed this to be the case when he saw her there, eyebrows perched and teeth glimmering in his direction.

OK, yes, I know what you might be thinking, but I promise there is a reason I wrote this example in such a wordy way. First of all, this form of storytelling, which is commonly referred to as "omniscient," isn't really an all-knowing form, but simply a more privileged one with access to more sides of the story. There's a very fine and confusing line between writing in **third person omniscient** and **head-hopping**. And third person omniscient is a very common excuse for the mistake of head-hopping.

So, what is the difference?

Well, a third person omniscient narrator should feel like a completely **separate entity with its own voice**, who knows retrospective information about the characters and the story, but they cannot tell you what the characters are thinking or feeling at any given point. They can only assume this, or give supporting information as to why they think this is true. Think of the third person omniscient narrator as a very concrete person, a character of its own, with an extremely distinct voice. Commonly, this type of narrator can be used when you have a character retelling events of a story that happened in their past, but trying to keep themselves completely out of it.

This is a very advanced technique and is extremely difficult to nail down, so don't worry if this seems too complex. There's still a huge array of positions you can choose! And if you wish to be in more characters' heads at once, you should revisit third person focalized, but remember to add scene or chapter breaks each time you switch the focus character to avoid head-hopping.

Tenses

Typically, stories are told in past tense, but there's been a rising number of books written in present tense in modern fiction, a narrative choice which is largely present in young adult (YA) novels.

At the end of the day, it's up to you what you choose, but keep in mind your reader's suspension of disbelief here as well. It's a minor distinction, but stories in past tense will immediately be more immersive than ones in present tense, simply because it's how we've always told stories. When we hear "Once upon a time, there was a kingdom . . ." we immediately know we're being told a narrative of something that happened, and we're able to easily believe everything we hear. This is much more difficult to achieve with a first person present tense narrator. Unless you're using devices such as letters and emails to write your present-narrator story, you run the risk of confusing your readers and making your story sound strained and unnatural.

Of course, when used in the right situations, present tense can be very effective. For example, some mystery or thriller novels can benefit from a fully present narrator to keep the suspense stronger, as the narrator doesn't have a way of knowing what will happen next. Their reactions and thoughts are not influenced by their future selves. Meanwhile, past tense can be great for narratives in which you wish to explore afterthoughts and retrospective internal monologues, as the past tense immediately distances the narrator from the character; we can imagine the narrator is the protagonist in the future, and has therefore had time to reflect on the events that happened, which means they can construct more immersive commentary on the events of the book.

In conclusion, you should choose the point of view that's best suited for your specific story. Think about the feeling you're trying to create for your readers, then use the narrative perspective as your first step toward that feeling.

Writing Prose

If you're a first-time writer, actually writing your ideas down into words, paragraphs and chapters can feel like you have absolutely no idea what you're doing. Writing prose is definitely a muscle you should be exercising as often as you can. If you're scared of having a bad writing style, then the absolute best way to improve is by reading lots and lots of books, especially those in the genre you're hoping to write in.

An unfortunate thing I see with many new writers is that they refuse to read anything for fear of being influenced by other works and then not being original enough themselves. This is a horribly limiting belief, and if you experience this yourself, I can promise you that writing a good book will be that much more difficult for you. All artists have influences, such is the nature of art! And your mind will never be truly untainted by other works of art. If you've watched any films, listened to any music or seen any paintings, I'm afraid you've already been influenced. Books are just another form of art, and there is an insurmountable amount of knowledge to gain from reading other authors' work. You will only get so far with words if you stick to your own little pool of knowledge, which will never expand unless you actually dive into bigger waters to learn more.

Now, I can't tell you how to write well; writing is art and, therefore, subjective as well as completely different across styles and genres. But I can give you some general guidelines to developing stronger prose if you're just starting out.

- Vary your sentence structure and rhythm.
- Stick to active sentences instead of passive. (*A mosquito bit me* instead of *I was bitten by a mosquito.*)
- The quicker you can get to your point, the better!

- Chitchat and mundane actions that add nothing to your plot or your characters are never necessary. (Dressing up, eating breakfast or moving between locations is not needed unless something crucial happens during those moments that impacts your story.)
- Avoid filter words, especially in close narrative perspectives. (See, feel, taste, know, seem, notice, smell, etc.)
- Mix different sections of prose.

I divide the different sections of prose into action, sensory description, narration, internal monologue and dialogue to make it easier to differentiate and practice each one. Let's dive into them.

Action
She slipped on a patch of ice while walking across the porch.

Action is a very simple part of prose that describes what your characters are doing at the present moment. Action is something you'll often interweave with other types of prose.

Sensory Description
The porch was covered in ice, and the frosty air bit at her cheeks. Her grandmother's cabin stood lonely in the mist of the white forest, the pleasant scent of fireplace smoke coming out in wisps from the stone chimney.

Sensory description is a writer's attempt to create vivid imagery and immerse readers into their story world. When crafting description like this, think of using more than just your visual senses. Include sounds, smells, tastes and tactile sensations.

Internal Monologue

She couldn't wait to get into the warm cabin. The cold wind had been carrying her thoughts off in different directions since leaving the town. Would anyone notice she'd gone? Her father would send a patrol if she didn't call him back soon. I best ask grandma for a phone as soon as I get in, *she thought.*

Internal monologue is used when you allow your character's thoughts to seep into the prose. You can use this subtly and weave it into your description, or you can input your character's thoughts directly into the paragraphs.

Narration

It was a chilly day in late December when she stepped up on the porch to visit her grandmother. She still remembers the thud of her backside hitting the wood after she slipped on the ice, and her grandma's sweet chuckle at the incident.

Narration is a bit of a mix of action and internal monologue, and I include it here as its own type because it's something I commonly use and tend to write a little differently than I would other types of prose. Narration is recalling a memory or retelling a story in short strides but filtering it through your character's voice and emotions for the event.

Dialogue

"Grandma? A little help!" she called from the ground.

Her grandmother opened the door and laughed. "Oh, you klutz. Should have told me you were coming, I would have shoveled the porch."

Dialogue is exactly what it sounds like, an exchange of words between your characters. Good dialogue depends highly on the uniqueness of your character voices, and will be significantly easier to come up with the better you know who these people are.

Notice that each of these pieces do their own job, but when used together they create a much stronger and more fleshed-out sense of your story.

Dialogue Hacks

Here are some actionable tips you can try out right now to improve any dialogue-heavy scene in your book. Keep in mind that while these are good hacks, they do require practice, and they'll never be able to replace the power of a good character voice. Use them mindfully.

Power of Silence

Silence is a tool that a lot of writers underestimate. Let's look at the difference in the following scenes.

Example #1

A: Why didn't you tell me?

B: I'm sorry, I just didn't feel I needed to tell you.

A: You should have told me! We could have gotten through it together.

B: Maybe I didn't want that.

A: You didn't want what?

B: I didn't want your help!

A: What do you mean by that?

B: You know what I mean.

A: It wasn't my help you needed, was it?

B: You know that, too.

Example #2

A: Why didn't you tell me?

B: Please, stop . . .

A: You could have told me! We could have gotten through this together.

B: . . .

A: Why didn't you tell me?

B: . . .

A: You didn't want my help. Did you?

B: . . .

A: You wanted his.

B: . . .

A: Right . . . OK. I get the picture.

Both of these scenes come from the same conflict, but they're vastly different in tone between the characters.

Silence can be really powerful in scenes of betrayal, or in scenes where one character is on the "attack" and the "victim" doesn't respond. This can be because they don't want to be having the conversation (usually due to the feeling of guilt), they don't want to play into the argument, they don't know how to gather their words or they're simply too terrified to speak.

Less Is More

Sometimes fixing up your dialogue can be as simple as cutting down the amount of words you put into it. For this hack, think about the rhythm of the conversation. Let's look at two examples.

Example #1

A: Are you free for dinner tonight?

B: Sorry, I can't really do tonight.

A: Are you saying you can't or you don't want to?

Example #2

A: Dinner tonight?

B: Can't.

A: Can't or won't?

Beyond just being so much easier to read, the latter example makes us feel as though the characters know each other better than the characters in the first example. It's a simple change, it improves the rhythm and readability, and it adds to your characters without taking away any information.

Voice Contrasts

This hack ties closely with your character voices. If you have two characters who are very different by nature—and so their voices and manner of speaking are different as well—this will make your dialogue a lot more dynamic. These types of distinctions are great for **creating conflict** within the scene and within the dialogue, too. Think about:

- the character who likes the sound of his own voice speaking to one who tends to shy away from conversations
- an intellectual character with a wide range of vocabulary speaking to a character with an extremely limited vocabulary
- a shy son and talkative mother
- an extroverted customer and quiet server
- a child full of questions and an adult grump

Ping-Pong Games

Think of your dialogue as a game of Ping-Pong. Try to keep your back-and-forths going for as long as they remain interesting, instead of cutting them off.

The Ping-Pong technique can be a really good way to approach writing arguments. The point of the game is to score the winning blow. Use that technique with your words.

If you have two people arguing, you want the blows to progressively get worse, up until the point where one of them takes it too far and strikes the winning blow. They might say something the other never expected to hear. They might say something they never meant to, but only said it because they knew it would hurt the most, and they were desperate to win that game. They might also dig out something from the other character's past and use it against them.

However.

The Ping-Pong technique doesn't necessarily need to be used exclusively for fights or arguments.

You can get really creative with this one. Think about:

- two characters trying to outsmart each other
- two characters who enjoy playful banter and pretend fights
- two characters gossiping (Which one can come up with the meanest retort over the person they're gossiping about?)
- two characters both feigning to be victims of the other

The Ping-Pong game can be a useful tool to create a dynamic conversation, to add rhythm and to make your scenes progressively more dramatic. This is a great exercise to reduce your amount of info dumping. Give your character a point they want to get to during a conversation. Then, have them say anything but. Let's look at these examples:

Before

A: So, how was class?

B: A snoozefest as usual. Mrs. Johnson divided us into groups for the semester.

A: Ah, who'd you get?

B: Anna, and the twin nerds.

A: Anna? Wait that means that you can—

B: —find out if she has a crush on you, yes.

A: Awesome.

After

A: So, how was class?

B: A snoozefest as usual. Mrs. Johnson divided us into groups for the semester.

A: Ah, who'd you get?

B: Anna, and the twin nerds.

A: Oh. Anna. Cool. Sc you're gonna be working with them for the next three months?

B: Yes. So, basically, no work for me. You know how the twins are.

A: Sure. Will you have group meetings?

B: Maybe.

A: I guess you'll be talking to those three a lot then, huh?

B: I suppose so.

A: You'll probably get to know them quite well.

B: Mhm.

A: I mean you'll probably discuss more than just school . . .

B: Yep.

A: Like who's got a crush on whom—

B: Is there something you want me to ask Anna?

A: I have no idea what you're insinuating.

The latter example becomes much more interesting to follow, and it adds a layer of depth to both of your characters' personalities. In the second example, character A is obviously the type who struggles asking for things or being upfront, whereas character B seems to be a joker who enjoys torturing character A by not playing along with their obvious insinuations. In the first example, you don't see any of these aspects.

The Third Character Trick

The third character trick is awesome when you want to explore your characters' personalities and make their conversations more awkward. The third character provides a great constriction of what can and can't be said during the exchange.

So, what is it? The third character is a person in the scene who isn't involved in the conversation but serves as an obstacle or a distraction.

If you want to make your characters more uncomfortable, or you want to find a way to make their dialogue more interesting by having to nitpick what to say before they say it, introducing the third character is a really fun way to achieve that.

Consider:

- A chirpy waitress interrupting a serious conversation between your characters. Perhaps your two characters are talking about robbing a supermarket. One of them is close to having a nervous breakdown, while the other is trying to keep them together. The waitress can serve as an added conflict, interrupting the panic-stricken characters to engage in normal chitchat, which is the last thing on their minds. She can also add motivation to the level-headed character, keeping the anxious one from blurting out anything too suspicious.

- A kid in the back seat of a car while his parents aim to pretend like they didn't just have a divorce-inducing fight moments before getting into the car. How will the parents speak about this elephant in the room without giving away the true source of their conversation to their child? Their predicament and their fight become much more interesting when you introduce the conflict of a third character, because they act as a strain on the conversation, so your characters will have to work within the confines of this added limitation.

Use the Setting as Opposition

This is a really easy trick to add some dimension and conflict to your dialogue. Think about what the conversation needs to be, and then think about the very worst place this conversation could happen—and then make it so.

- Imagine a life-changing conversation during which one of the characters gets really angry, but set it in a tiny canoe in the middle of the night, too far from shore to swim out if it were to tip over.

- Write a must-tell gossip, but set it during a funeral, and the gossip is so juicy the characters can't stop whispering amongst themselves.

- Brainstorm a sensitive conversation about the fate of a relationship, and then set it in the middle of a live concert.

SHOW DON'T TELL AND THE TEMPTATION OF INFO DUMPING

Info dumping is a really easy trap to fall into when writing dialogue. Let's first get a good grasp on what info dumping covers:

- Character revealing too much backstory
- Character explaining their feelings
- Character explaining their mood
- Characters talking about a plot point that's necessary for the story, but that they would never realistically talk about
- Characters saying absolutely anything without a specific reason to say it. If you cannot answer "Why would they say that in this situation?" with a logical answer, it might mean that dialogue is an info dump.

So, how do we avoid these?

There's one trick you need to master in order to rule the kingdom of info dump–less writing. (That's a word, right?) This trick is very simple:

Give your readers some credit.

The reason we fall onto the crutch of info dumping is that we believe the readers won't get it otherwise. Don't think of your readers as idiots. It's as simple as that. They don't need everything spelled out for them. And sometimes they don't even need to know everything, they just need to feel it.

If you're describing a really heartbreaking moment of betrayal between two characters, the scene might be even more powerful if the reader doesn't know exactly what happened or exactly what the two are talking about. They might assume things and find out what happened later in the story, or they might never find out at all. As long as you convey the emotion of betrayal, they'll feel the heartbreak, and at the end of that day, that's all that matters.

Now, "**show don't tell**" is a very popular phenomenon among writers that everyone tells you to pay special attention to, but it's rarely ever explained. It goes hand in hand with info dumping. But what does it actually apply to?

The general rule I like to stick to is simply *tell the external stuff and show the internal stuff*.

There are things you're better off telling instead of showing.

An excellent way of mastering your "show don't tell" skills is the use of **subtext**. You can craft subtext in most scenes of your story from the way your characters act, which actions they take and even what words they use. Here are some of my best tips to curb your info dumps and your over-telling:

- Enter into the scene late (when an incident has already happened and we only get to witness the aftermath, without too much context) or leave the scene early (before we know how it resolves, so we can fill in the gaps ourselves from the context of the following scenes/chapters).

- When writing dialogue, ask yourself what info your characters are already aware of, because this is something you should omit. A lot of dialogue is often written only for the reader's benefit and isn't something your characters would naturally say.

- Don't assume your reader needs to know everything in order to understand your story. The less you can tell them while still allowing them to follow along, the more intrigue you create.

- Emotions should always be there to be assumed and figured out based on context and subtext, not explained. Try not to use emotion descriptors such as sighs of frustration, tears of joy, nervous chuckles or the like. Leave them as expressionless sighs, tears through bright eyes and shaky chuckles instead.

- Most conversations can have a hidden motive for all parties involved. Go into each scene of dialogue with a specific goal in mind for the characters involved, and think of how to get them to achieve this goal without ever directly asking about it.

THE OPENING

The opening of your book is a crucial thing to get right. You probably already know of the importance of a good hook, the gripping first page and strong opening chapter. This is the make-or-break section of your novel. This is when a potential reader will decide whether they're invested in the story, will purchase your book and continue to devour it page by page because they just need to know what happens, or they'll shrug their shoulders and put the book right back on the shelf.

So, how can you make sure your book doesn't get tossed back onto the shelves and forgotten? How can you make sure your story is interesting enough to be picked up? There's one key answer to this.

You have to make the reader care.

Those first few pages of a book should never be wasted on setting a scene, explaining the world, exploring legends, backstories or easing the reader into the action of your story world. When the reader first picks up your book, the moment they open it, they know nothing about it. But this is not an excuse to throw this information at them and clear up the type of story you're going to be telling or the world you're going to be telling it in. This simply doesn't matter to your reader. At this point, they will not care.

What you want them to feel after reading the first page or two is the connection to the **character** who's carrying the story, and an interest in whatever journey this character is taken on. So, what is the one crucial part of the opening to your book, the one key thing that you should make the reader immediately aware of, the one simple way that you can make them instantly care for what happens to this character?

You do this by introducing their internal conflict.

Don't save that internal struggle for later. Don't be tempted to keep your protagonist a mystery. Your readers *need* to know what this character is struggling with in order to actually care about them. So, the sooner you can tell readers about the predicament the characters have found themselves in, the better. And this predicament should never be solely external. Remember the one thing that keeps your readers hooked is the knowledge of your hero's flaw, struggle or misbelief. Or, in other words, the ways in which they're the ones holding themselves back from fulfillment.

PROLOGUES AND WHETHER YOU NEED ONE

Should your story have a prologue? A prologue is the opening scene of your book, and it's not considered to be a chapter. It's there to set the scene and raise questions, to hook the readers and make them want to know how this story continues. You can think of it as a mini trailer or a sneak peek of your narrative. Prologues can also be written in a different narrative perspective from the rest of your book.

A good prologue can be:
- A sneak peek into the action
- A hint at the conflict
- An important scene that might tie into the story later
- A relevant backstory or predating event that raises a story question

What your prologue should do:
- Hook your reader
- Make them ask questions
- Be short and concise
- Set up the story question and/or conflict of your book

What your prologue shouldn't do:
- Info dump
- Give us irrelevant backstory
- Lay out all the world-building details for us
- Be long

So, before you jump into it, determine whether your story actually needs a prologue. If you're only planning to use it to give your reader information about your story, scratch that idea right now.

If you want a good example of a prologue, have a look at *The Secret History* by Donna Tartt or *The Book Thief* by Markus Zusak.

THE FIRST CHAPTER CHECKLIST

- ☐ Set the scene with action
- ☐ Write an intriguing first paragraph
- ☐ Introduce the protagonist
- ☐ Establish the narrative perspective
- ☐ Set the genre
- ☐ Hint at themes or pose the story question
- ☐ Paint a clear picture of the protagonist's world
- ☐ Introduce the protagonist's flaws
- ☐ Foreshadow the inciting incident
- ☐ Keep a good chapter structure
- ☐ End on a cliff-hanger or intriguing last line

THE MIDDLE

The middle of a book is a notoriously dark void. Most writers will say they know the beginning and the end of their story, but the middle is one big blur. If you are struggling with this issue yourself, then the How to Plan Your Novel chapter of this guide (see page 82) may have helped steer you in the right direction, and hopefully you gained some clarity on this.

My biggest piece of advice on overcoming this issue is to **not race to the end**. It can be so tempting to try to resolve everything that happens as soon as possible, especially if you put your characters through a grueling pit of misery and you want to make them happy again. But this is where you need to resist that urge. Allowing your characters time to struggle and time to grow is where the peak of storytelling comes from.

Honestly, the key trick to write a strong middle of your story is **the midpoint**.

Think of your story as having **two parts**: the first story is everything leading up to the midpoint, which is where you flip everything on its head and you begin the second story. Having a strong midpoint is absolutely crucial to pacing out your novel so you don't only have a beginning, a meek rise of action and a resolution.

Remember, your **inciting incident should prompt your first external goal**, which is what your hero will be chasing throughout the first part of your story. Once you reach the midpoint, **you can change the goal** to something completely different. Perhaps your character finally got close enough to see their external goal and you reveal to them that it's been a farce all along, and they really should have been chasing something different. This is how you **prompt your secondary external goal** and get more flesh to your story.

Remember to use your middle to build out:

- your story world
- your character relationships
- each individual character journey
- rising obstacles
- possible answers to your story questions
- the themes of your story

THE PERFECT ENDING
HOW TO FIND YOUR HAPPY (OR UNHAPPY) END

Now that you've dealt with the majority of your story, it's time to detangle all those issues that your characters inevitably created along the way. Typically, all these resolutions will relate closely to your character journeys (which I hope you've thought about).

Not all the resolutions need to be happy. We've touched on this briefly when we spoke of negative character arcs and your character journeys. Usually, you'll have one of three types of endings:

- Happy
- Tragic
- Bittersweet

And these can also vary among plot strings and different characters—meaning your hero's story could end happily, while the secondary protagonist could have a bittersweet ending.

Happy Endings

Happy endings for your characters should always involve that character **achieving their internal goal**—overcoming their flaw or their struggle, and growing as a person. They may or may not achieve the external goal; this isn't always necessary. For example, by achieving their internal goal, they might find they no longer need or care for their external one.

Bittersweet Endings

Bittersweet endings happen when your character achieves either only their internal goal or only their external one. Remember, not achieving their external goal doesn't automatically mean it's a bittersweet ending—it can still be a happy one if your hero decides that they didn't need their external goal. But if their external goal was something extremely important to them, the ending might still feel bittersweet. It's all about your character's attitude.

However, in the case of them achieving their external goal but not their internal, the ending will be bittersweet without a doubt. Sometimes more bitter than sweet. This could imply that they put themselves on the backburner, sacrificed their own needs or their own progress for the greater good. Or they simply refused to learn from their mistakes and forced the accomplishment of the external goal through all the wrong mediums, and therefore didn't achieve any internal change.

Bittersweet endings are great for series of books, because your readers will know your characters still have something to learn or something to accomplish.

Tragic Endings

Tragic endings are very simply ones where your character achieves neither of their goals. They never learn from their mistakes, they never change and they never accomplish what they set out to do.

ALL ABOUT EPILOGUES

Most books don't need an epilogue. But if yours could fit one, we're going to go over what a good epilogue should look like.

What is an epilogue? An epilogue is a conclusion at the end of your novel, but it is **not an essential part of the story**. An epilogue should be a **bonus**, but not a crucial part of the book.

It is important to note that you can change your POV for the epilogue. (For example, if your book was in first person, your epilogue can be in third person.) You can also use it as a framed narrative with your prologue and keep a consistent approach to both. For example, *Shadow and Bone* by Leigh Bardugo links the prologue and epilogue by using a third person narrator to tell the beginning and end of the story of her two main characters. This acts as a framing device for the story that's told in first person.

An epilogue can be used for two purposes:

- **Provide a sense of closure.** Wrap up your loose ends, and give your reader a look into how things resolved for your hero. Usually, it would be set in the future and work as a short bonus story that showcases how your hero is getting on in their *new equilibrium*.
- **Hint at a sequel.** If you're writing a series, an epilogue could be a good place to add a minor hint of an unresolved story line, one that could potentially evolve into a threat for your hero in the future.

What an epilogue shouldn't do:

- Overexplain the end of your story, or the meaning behind it
- Be used as a cliff-hanger (you can hint at future issues and set up new possibilities for the next installment of your story if writing a series, but don't leave the epilogue unfinished)
- Be used as the ending (you should already have a strong ending; remember: the epilogue is a bonus)

MINDSET AND CONFIDENCE
IDENTIFYING AND OVERCOMING WRITER'S BLOCK

As a writer, you must have heard tons about writer's block. They talk about it in movies, you hear people say it when they get stuck on any written projects, you've probably said it yourself: "Ah, I'm just going through a bit of a writer's block at the moment."

But why do we say this so often?

Probably because it's easier to blame a vague concept that befalls all writers than to figure out why you're getting stuck and take the responsibility yourself. Here are the three biggest reasons you might have experienced writer's block.

#1 Lack of Clarity

This is the absolute most common reason people get stuck in their project and blame it on writer's block. They actually just don't have clarity on their project; they haven't planned enough, they haven't fleshed out their characters and they have no idea where their story is actually going or what it is they are writing about. So, ask yourself these questions:

- Do I know my hero? Do I know what they want and what they need to learn?

- Do I have a strong theme and message behind my story? Do I know why I'm writing this?

- Do I have an outline? Do I follow story structure and know what's going to happen in my book before I set out to write it?

- What about the rest of my characters? Do I know them? Do I know what drives them? Do they all have a specific purpose in the story?

- Do I have an idea of my chapter structure? Do I know roughly how many chapters I will have and what each of them should be about?

If you answered no to at least one of these questions, you need to get clearer on your story.

#2 Lack of Passion

Lack of passion for a project sometimes actually stems from a lack of clarity. This means you might not have a theme/message behind your story, or you might not have fleshed out your characters enough; you might not have given your characters a big enough purpose to fulfill, or a big enough reason to exist.

How do you get passionate about your story? You need to know why you're telling it. You need to have a burning desire to tell it—because you know no one besides you can. And if you don't, it will die with you, and that idea should be unbearable.

When we create projects, they should become our children. We should care about them in an almost maternal way, and we should want to shape them into the best version of themselves before we let them out into the world.

Being involved and passionate about your story is the number one drive you're going to need to finish it.

If you're lacking the passion, ask yourself:

- Am I writing this story for a reason? Can I define that reason?
- Do I know exactly what I'm trying to say with this story and why I'm trying to say it?
- Does my protagonist have a strong enough motivation?
- Am I dying to tell my protagonist's story?
- Did I flesh out the rest of my characters enough so that they have a role to play in my story?

#3 Mindset

The last reason is the most difficult one to tackle. But it is something we overlook a lot.

How do *you* feel? Where is your head at?

This has absolutely nothing to do with your writing, your project, your outline, your passion or anything else. This is about your general state of mind. You cannot expect to be creative if you're feeling mentally exhausted or unfulfilled. Mental health is obviously something you should be working toward either way, and you might have days where you feel great and being creative comes easily, but there might be days where you feel like crap and nothing could push you to create. What you need to do is recognize when one of these days comes around. And when you're aware that the reason you're unable to create is because your mental health is in the gutter, that is when you should forgive yourself.

Hitting yourself in the head over being unable to write is not going to help you; it will only force you to stay in that gutter for longer. Which is why you should train yourself to recognize times where writing isn't possible and let them go, rather than despairing and guilt-tripping yourself, because it's only going to drive you deeper into the gutter.

It's perfectly normal to feel this way. It's perfectly normal to have times where creativity seems impossible. So, learn to be aware of these times, and learn to accept them.

ACTIONABLE METHODS TO KEEP YOU WRITING

Now, let's move on to some actionable things you can do to keep yourself motivated as a writer. Notice I use the word motivation, and never inspiration? Let me quickly explain why.

You don't necessarily need inspiration to write. That's a damaging idea that can seriously hold you back from being creative. Inspiration is amazing when it happens, but it's not something most of us can afford to wait for, and that does include you, too.

Motivation, on the other hand, I think of as a completely different concept, and it's something you can learn to nurture. It comes from your willpower, and from a nurturing lifestyle. Logically, if you take care of your health, if you're well-rested and hydrated and well-fed, you're way more likely to feel motivated to work and be passionate about your projects, too.

Here are some little actionable tips you can implement into your day-to-day writing routine that will help you keep up the motivation to work.

Frame Your Best Quotes

Consider this as you write: You must have had moments when you came up with a really amazing sentence, paragraph or quote that you're very proud of. Each time this happens, go ahead and write it down somewhere. Start a collection of your favorite quotes, written by you (not by a random author or motivational guru online), and this is a sure way to boost your confidence as a writer. Read these back when you feel low, and remind yourself that this is what you're capable of.

Celebrate Small Victories

Congratulate yourself every time you finish a chapter. Every time you finish a page. Keep looking back at where you started and how far you've come. Try to teach yourself to appreciate your own growth. It's going to go a long way in knowing your self-worth. Don't look at your first five chapters as "just five chapters," look at them as an amazing solid start to your story.

Keep in mind that more than 90 percent of writers tend not to get past their first chapter. Every added chapter puts you farther ahead in your journey and should be celebrated. It's not a common thing. It really isn't. Not everyone can stay consistent with one project and finish it. In fact, most people can't. But you're still here. Celebrate that.

Type with Your Screen Covered

This is a neat trick that might help you with:

- Not editing as you write
- Not keeping track of your word count
- Not wasting time rereading what you wrote so far, and instead focusing on simply writing

This is a really great way to consider writing up your first draft, just to get those words out on the page and not worry too much about the details. Consider turning off your monitor or covering your screen so you are unable to see the words you're typing or the word count you're hitting.

Use the Power of Writing Sprints (Even When You're Alone)

If you know me, you know I'm a massive advocate for writing sprints, and you might want me to shut up about it already. But the reason I stand behind it is because it works.

During a sprint of fifteen minutes, you can usually average between 300 to 600 words. So, having an hour in your day and doing four of these sprints means you can end up with 1,000 to 2,000 new words on the page.

You can do writing sprints with other writers (for some added pressure and accountability), but you should also teach yourself to do them alone.

Just set a timer, start it and write. Rinse and repeat.

Save the Good Feedback

Ever gotten feedback by a writing professional? A teacher? A friend with a keen eye on literature? Has any of it made your heart feel warm? If so, save it.

Any time you get good feedback that reminds you of why you started writing, save it somewhere (just like your best quotes) and use it to get inspired and be reminded of the reason you're doing this.

Dissect Your Old Writing to See How Far You've Come

This is a very interesting method you can use to give yourself some confidence. Think about whether you have any old writing you would be ashamed to show to anyone today, then read it and see if you can criticize it from your current perspective. It might just show you how far you've come and that you're able to recognize your own mistakes.

Find a Writing Program That Inspires You

If your old Google Doc is a little bit boring and monotone, consider the novelty of a writing program crafted specifically for authors. There are many options out there to choose from, so do some research and see which one might suit you best.

Are you the type that loves plotting tools? Do you love formatting text to make it look like a publishable piece? Do you like the clickity-clackity noises of keys as you type? Or are you a minimalist, and you need as simple of an interface as possible, preferably full-screen? Whatever type of writer you are, there's sure to be a writing software you can connect with.

WRITING EXERCISES

- **Stuck in a scene with a certain character?** It might be because you don't know them well enough. Step away from the scene, and figure out their individual motivation behind whatever conversation or mission they are on. If there is no clear reason for them being in this scene, make one, or give them a hidden agenda.

- **Scene falling flat?** Try adding a sudden change in weather, like a hailstorm or a thunderstorm.

- **Is your prose just not quite coming out today?** Write out the rest of your scene or chapter using only the dialogue exchanges. Express any actions and important moments outside of dialogue with a few words you can make sense of later.

* **Feeling a bit bored with your current dialogue?** Amp up the conflict. If the characters in your scene are getting along and agreeing on things, then there's likely nothing to explore there. Create a divide between them. A differing of opinions on a certain topic can be more than enough to do the trick and turn a boring conversation interesting.

* **Are you struggling to find the right words to express what you want to write about?** Write absolute gibberish instead. If you're really struggling with a paragraph, allow yourself to still write it out by using the first words that pop into your mind. Chances are, you could still nail the sentence structure or emotion you were going for. You can clean up the details later.

* **Does your chapter feel boring?** Take another look at it and see if things might be going a little too well for your character. Are you simply getting them from point A to point B of your plot with no complications? This won't do! Throw some obstacles in there, and make the journey harder for them.

* **Intimidated by the last few lines on your document?** Step away from the computer, and try writing your next scene by hand, resuming from memory.

* **Do you feel like you're losing the connection with your protagonist?** Write a scene that reminds them of the extent of their motive. Why did they set out on this journey in the first place, what's pushing them onward and why do they care about achieving this? If this feels like a difficult thing to think about, you likely don't have clear character motivations.

* **Is your sensory description falling flat?** Try visiting a unique public space where you can sit and write in the moment. What do you see? Describe the colors. Are there any sounds, and what do they remind you of? What can you smell? What can you touch, and how does it feel under your palm?

ONWARD

I think it's safe to say you're more than ready to begin your journey as a writer. One thing I'd like to encourage you to do if you haven't already begun writing your project, is to do so as soon as possible. As helpful as this book might be, and as important as having an outline of your novel is, you don't want to get stuck in the planning without ever putting any words down on paper.

Writing is a constant process of learning and change. And you have to actually write in order to discover new things about your story and characters, or you will simply remain stuck in the same spot. If you've followed this book, you've got the bones of your story all laid out. The skeleton is there, but it's up to you to connect it, to build out the flesh and the rest of the body (no *Frankenstein* references intended).

As you know now, writing is not a hobby of instant gratification, and it's not something anyone else can do for you. So, remember the vision of your project and the reason you need it to be out there. Grab your outlines for reference, and get going.

No one else can tell this story as well as you can.

If you ever get stuck, you can always revisit this book and trace your steps back to the foundations, or even use it to start your next project, and the one after that!

ACKNOWLEDGMENTS

I want to start this by thanking the team over at the Kinloch Hotel, which was the place that allowed me to heal from so many things that I have been carrying with me for years, and gave me the strength to pursue a writing career.

To Gemma, Robbie, Barbara, Su, Andrew, Russell, Lauren, Laura, Charlotte, Fraser, Jenna, Kayleigh and Catriona for creating a space where I could flourish.

Thanks to my partner in crime, Kai Wissler, for supporting me and believing in me for years, and for inadvertently coming up with my company name and letting me use it free of charge.

Thank you to Barbara Szép, as my first employee, for holding me up when times got tough, and to Jasmina Coric, my second employee, for lifting my spirits with bad jokes.

Thanks to my mom, dad, brother and grandma for letting me do my own thing and trusting that I'd do it right or else learn from my mistakes.

Thanks to my editor, Madeline Greenhalgh, for shaping my vague ideas and general assumptions into cohesive chapters, for making sure I'm not embarrassing myself (much) and for elevating this book into a sensible read I can say I'm proud of.

Thanks to Pamela and Thomas over at Novlr for believing in my potential enough to partner with me, when I was only just starting out. And of course, the greatest of thank-yous to all my clients and students, who supported me in this journey and helped me learn more about the craft of writing than I could have ever known before them.

ABOUT THE AUTHOR

Char Anna is a writer based in Scotland, a fiction writing coach and the creator of The Plottery—a service-based business helping authors write and grow. She became independent at the age of 17, when she moved from her home country of Croatia to the United Kingdom, supporting herself through a bachelor's degree in filmmaking and screenwriting from University of the West of Scotland, as well as a master's in creative writing from Edinburgh Napier University. Char founded The Plottery at the beginning of 2022 while working full-time in a family-owned hotel on the Isle of Arran, with the intent of creating a community for writers that made it easy for anyone to write a book, no matter their level of experience in the storytelling industries. The Plottery grew rapidly with its signature coaching program, Power Plotter, and Char's online course for writers, Novel Plotting Academy, which now teaches hundreds of writers.

INDEX